FEMINIST READINGS / SERIES EDITOR: SUE ROE

Nathaniel Hawthorne

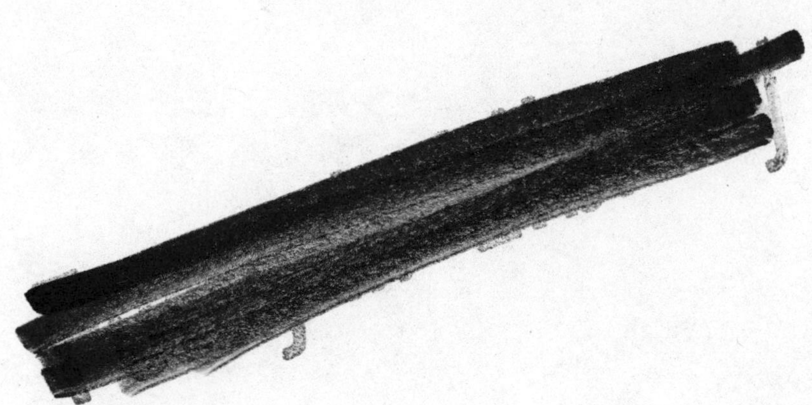

By the same author

Virginia Woolf's First Voyage: A Novel in the Making (Macmillan, London; Rowman and Littlefield, Totowa, New Jersey, 1984)

Melymbrosia by Virginia Woolf: An Early Version of The Voyage Out (The New York Public Library, New York, 1982)

Between Women: Biographers, Novelists, Critics, Teachers, and Artists Write about Their Work on Women (with Carol Ascher and Sara Ruddick) (Beacon, Boston, 1984)

The Letters of Vita Sackville-West to Virginia Woolf (with Mitchell A. Leaska) (Hutchinson, London, and Morrow, New York, 1984)

FEMINIST READINGS / SERIES EDITOR: SUE ROE

Nathaniel Hawthorne

LOUISE DESALVO

Professor of English
Hunter College of The City University of New York

HUMANITIES PRESS INTERNATIONAL, INC.
Atlantic Highlands, NJ

First published in 1987 in the United States of America by
HUMANITIES PRESS INTERNATIONAL, INC.,
Atlantic Highlands, NJ 07716

Library of Congress Cataloging-in-Publication Data

DeSalvo, Louise A., 1942–
Nathaniel Hawthorne.

(Feminist readings)
Bibliography: p.
Includes index.
1. Hawthorne, Nathaniel, 1804–1864—Characters—Women. 2. Women in Literature. 3. Sex in literature. 4. Feminism and literature—United States. I. Title. II. Series.
PS1892.W6D47 1987 813′.3 86–30022
ISBN 0–391–03512–6
ISBN 0–391–03513–4 (pbk.)

PRINTED IN GREAT BRITAIN

For Carol Smith

who first taught me how to read men's texts
from a woman's point of view

Feminist Readings

Series Editor: Sue Roe

The *Feminist Readings* series has been designed to investigate the link between literary writing and feminist reading by surveying the key works of English Literature by male authors from new feminist perspectives.

Working from a position which accepts that the notion of gender difference embraces interrelationship and reciprocity as well as opposition, each contributor to the series takes on the challenge of reassessing the problems inherent in confronting a 'phallocentric' literary canon, by investigating the processes involved in the translation of gender difference into the themes and structures of the literary text.

Each volume surveys briefly the development of feminist literary criticism and the broader questions of feminism which have been brought to bear on this practice, from the initial identification of 'phallocentrism', through the tendency of early feminist critics to read literature as a sociological document, through to feminist criticism's current capacity to realign the discoveries of a wide range of disciplines in order to reassess theories of gender difference. The tendency of the feminist critic to privilege texts written by women and the notion that it might be possible to identify an autonomous tradition of 'women's writing' can offer a range of challenges to current feminist criticism, and the key texts by male authors surveyed by the series are considered in this light.

Can there be a politics of feminist criticism? How might a theory of sexual difference be seen to be directly applicable to critical practice? The series as a whole represents a comprehensive survey of the development of various theories of gender difference, and, by assessing their applicability to the writing of the most influential male writers of the literary tradition, offers a broadly revisionary interpretation of feminist critical practice.

Louise DeSalvo	*Nathaniel Hawthorne*
Bonnie Kime Scott	*James Joyce*
Julia Briggs	*Shakespeare*
Jacqueline Di Salvo	*Milton*
Sandra Gilbert	*T.S. Eliot*
Patricia Ingham	*Thomas Hardy*
Kate McLuskie	*Renaissance Dramatists*
Jill Mann	*Geoffrey Chaucer*
Marion Shaw	*Alfred Lord Tennyson*
Margarita Stocker	*Marvell*

Contents

Preface	xi
Acknowledgements	xvi
Chapter One: Nathaniel Hawthorne and feminists	1
Chapter Two: Feminists and Nathaniel Hawthorne	23
Chapter Three: *Fanshawe, A Tale* (1828)	39
Chapter Four: *The Scarlet Letter, A Romance* (1850)	57
Chapter Five: *The House of the Seven Gables* (1851)	77
Chapter Six: *The Blithedale Romance* (1852)	97
Epilogue	121
Notes	123
Select Bibliography	137
Index	148

Preface

In 1979, Professor Frank McLaughlin, my colleague at Fairleigh Dickinson University, where I was then teaching, suggested that I turn a number of my lectures about how literature acts as a form of enculturation into an article for *Media and Methods*, a journal he edited. 'Literature and sexuality: teaching the truth about the body', appeared in September 1979, and argued that Nathaniel Hawthorne's *The Scarlet Letter* (in addition to other works of literature) was being used by teachers in the United States as a covert means of warning young people about the perils of sexuality, the virtues of victimization, and the ennoblement of suffering and self-sacrifice.

The article expressed my belief that works of literature that become part of a canon, taught to virtually all students of literature in a given society, take on the quality of sacred texts which pass on to the next generation a set of beliefs and attitudes which the culture considers to be important. And, as with other forms of enculturation, this process occurs beyond the threshold of one's awareness. I believed that Nathaniel Hawthorne's *The Scarlet Letter* was one of those works.

The article was critical of a curriculum which taught only works in which sexuality is linked with incest, rape, murder, repression, violence, or victimization, and not works in which wholesome adults come to terms with themselves as sexual beings. It criticized the ways in which these works were taught—not as vehicles for unleashing inquiry into the organization of American society, but rather for tacitly accepting the social norms operating in these works.

I wondered why Hester Prynne (Hawthorne's heroine) was held up to young people (particularly to young women) as a model to emulate when, in the course of the novel, Hester became 'a self-ordained Sister of Mercy who turned from a life of feeling to a lonely existence filled with thought and self-sacrifice'.[1] There was a great danger, I thought, in glorifying Hester's suffering, and in romanticizing it. I wondered why students were taught that it was a tribute to Hester's character as a human being that she chose to stay close to her lover in a Puritan community which persecuted her. I wondered why her behaviour in the novel was applauded, rather than being understood as the only way a woman in her position could behave. Her self-abnegation was, for me, a tactic for survival—a criticism of the society which forced her to behave in this way—rather than a behaviour to emulate. I wondered why teachers were not able to discuss the thorny and complicated issue of how a society like that of Puritan America (and that of Hawthorne's time, as well) used norms of sexual behaviour as a means of enslaving its women and controlling them.

Like D. H. Lawrence, who called *The Scarlet Letter* 'an earthly story with a hellish meaning',[2] I believed that Hawthorne's attitude towards Hester Prynne revealed a great deal about the national temperament, about American male revulsion towards strong women, towards sexual women. Lawrence believed that American myths, which were, in turn, based upon Biblical myths, permitted the culture to blame its women for all the evil which exists in the world. He described how American men shifted the responsibility for their actions onto the women in their lives; how the national tendency to idolize women and idealize them masked a hidden terror of their power, and masked as well the fact that women, in reality, had virtually no political or economic power.

'Literature and sexuality' was but one of scores of articles written by feminists in the United States challenging the assumptions of a male-dominated literary establishment, which not only controlled *what* works of literature were taught in the nation's schools—largely works written by privileged white males—but also, *the ways* in which those works of literature were taught—as works of high culture, rather than as reflecting the misogyny, racism, classism, and homophobia that has been an integral part of the literary landscape in the United States. It signalled the beginning of my own preoccupation with the work of Nathaniel Hawthorne, and, more specifically, with how the portraits of women in the novels of Nathaniel Hawthorne reflect his own and his culture's ambivalence towards women, which often flares into overt misogyny. The writing of this book is the culmination of that concern.

In the meantime, my work on the process of the creation of Virginia Woolf's novels and on her relationship with Vita Sackville-West reinforced the idea that works of art are always a complex reaction to the society in which the writer lives, and that a writer's personal life is always reflected in the works that are created. What this book incorporates, as well, are the insights Woolf herself developed in works like *A Room of One's Own* which explore the relationship between economic and class privilege and the process of literary creation. Hawthorne attended Bowdoin College with the American counterparts of students at Oxbridge—men like Jonathan Cilley, Franklin Pierce, Horatio Bridge, and Oliver Wendell Holmes, who were the political and intellectual élite in the formative years of the American republic.[3] But Hawthorne was himself poor, although he was privileged in the sense that he was a white male and could attend a school like Bowdoin. He was, therefore, in many ways, as much an outsider as the young women attending Woolf's fictive Fernham College, and her insight that one 'cannot think well, love well, sleep well, if one has not dined well' is as applicable to a young man in Hawthorne's position in the United States as it was to those young women in Woolf's text who had to content themselves with plain gravy soup rather than the soles and partridges upon which their brothers at Oxbridge had feasted.

Nathaniel Hawthorne has been written for the student who wishes to explore and develop feminist approaches to and readings of the work of Nathaniel Hawthorne. The first chapter, 'Nathaniel Hawthorne and feminists', provides an introduction to Hawthorne's attitude towards feminism and to women, a fascinating and complicated issue which can only be sketched here. The second chapter, 'Feminists and Hawthorne', describes the scholarly and critical tradition within which this work is located, and major feminist criticism of Hawthorne. Each subsequent chapter treats one book-length major novel, or romance, published in his lifetime, in the order in which he wrote them: *Fanshawe: A Tale* (published in 1828, anonymously, and at his own expense); *The Scarlet Letter, A Romance* (1850); *The House of the Seven Gables* (1851); and *The Blithedale Romance* (1852). Because this study has been conceptualized as exploring Hawthorne's uneasy response to the movement for women's rights in the United States, *The Marble Faun* (1860), set in Italy, has not been taken up. Written after Hawthorne's appointment as American consul at Liverpool, and his lengthy sojourn in Europe, the characters' responses are, in the words of the critic John W. Bicknell, 'inseparable from Italy'.[4] Critics have described Hawthorne's description of Hilda in that novel as an example of 'innocent independence which an unchaperoned female could paradoxically enjoy in corrupt Rome' and of Miriam in that novel as being linked with women in the Old Testament, 'capable of violence in the primitive biblical exactions of the Mosaic law'.[5]

This work of feminist inquiry is dependent upon the scholarly tradition, both feminist and non-feminist, which I refer to throughout the text and which I gratefully acknowledge here. Considerable attention has been paid to describing Hawthorne criticism and scholarship to demonstrate the ways in which feminist criticism both depends upon and deviates from earlier work in a given field of inquiry. Feminist students of Hawthorne will discover, as I have, that the field of scholarship which has investigated nineteenth-century American society and its literature in the context of the experience of women and their representation in art is an enormously rich one. They will discover as well, that virtually every critic and scholar of Hawthorne's work develops an insight worth pursuing. In Hawthorne studies, the problem for the feminist student will be in reading all the relevant material, not in finding it.

Acknowledgements

I wish to acknowledge the help and support of Carol Ascher, Richard Barickman, Allan Brick, Marlies Danziger, Nancy Dean, Calvin Edwards, David Gordon, Karen Greenberg, Dorothy Helly, Alan Holder, Harriet Johnson, Wendell Johnson, Eve Leoff, Jane Lilienfeld, Nick Lyons, Frank McLaughlin, Audre Lorde, Lewis Meyers, Phyllis Moe, Regula Noetzli, Dennis Paoli, Charles Persky, Gerald Pinciss, Ann Raimes, Sara Ruddick, Susan Shapiro, Charlotte Sheedy, Catharine Stimpson, David Winn and Elizabeth Wood. I owe a special debt of gratitude to my editor, Sue Roe, for suggesting that I undertake this project and for seeing it through to its completion; David Leverenz, who helped me make my way through the field of Hawthorne scholarship; T. Walter Herbert, who sent me his essays before their publication; Joyce W. Warren, for allowing me to see the galleys of her book before its publication, and Leslie Mitchner, Senior Editor, Rutgers University Press, for sending them to me; Annette Kolodny, for her work and support; Jane Marcus, for continuing inspiration through the model of her own inquiry and for helping me pursue difficult lines of argument; Katherine Probst, for listening to and criticizing virtually every idea in this book; Blanche Weisen Cook, for providing a model of historical inquiry, and, even more importantly, a sustaining friendship; Jenny Palmer, for assisting me; President Donna Shalala, of Hunter College, for providing a haven within which feminist inquiry is rewarded and respected; and my students in Images of Women in American Literature, in Spring 1984 and 1985, who provided a spirited and lively forum within which I could try out many of the ideas presented here.

My husband, Ernest J. DeSalvo has, once again, helped me through the writing of a book, and this one, like the other ones, wouldn't have come into existence without him and his confidence that I could ultimately make sense. Our children, Jason and Justin, continue to be interested in my work, and I am grateful to them for it: it has been a pleasure to watch them read and react to the books that I myself have been writing about. My parents, Mildred and Louis Sciacchetano, continue to provide loving support.

Carol Smith, to whom this work is dedicated, provided a model of scholarship when I was her student at Douglass College in 1963, and she continues to be a source of inspiration still. I dedicate this book to her because she prompted many of the avenues of inquiry explored in this volume.

Stony Ridge
Sag Harbor, New York
1 August 1985

If ever I saw a man who combined delicate tenderness
to understand the heart of a woman, with
a quiet depth and manliness enough
to satisfy her, it is
Mr. Hawthorne.

Margaret Fuller to Sophia Peabody, 4 June 1841
on Sophia's marriage to Nathaniel Hawthorne

* * *

Old-fashioned Nathaniel, with his little-boy charm, he'll
tell you what's what. But he'll cover it with smarm.

D. H. Lawrence, *Studies in Classic American Literature*

CHAPTER ONE

Nathaniel Hawthorne and Feminists

The Scarlet Letter, the novel which marked the beginning of Nathaniel Hawthorne's fame as a writer, was published in 1850, just two years after the 1848 convention in Seneca Falls, New York, which 'marked the beginning of the political organization of women in their own behalf' in the United States.[1] The most important phase of Hawthorne's career—the period during which he composed *The Scarlet Letter, The House of the Seven Gables, The Blithedale Romance,* and *The Marble Faun*—therefore, coincided with the increasingly activist nineteenth-century political movement for women's rights.

In the course of his career as a writer and as a diplomat, Hawthorne himself personally knew many prominent nineteenth-century women who, either directly or indirectly, were connected with the feminist struggle for legal equity or with its companion movement, the abolitionist movement, women such as Harriet Martineau, Geraldine Jewsbury, Margaret Fuller (author of *Woman in the Nineteenth Century*), Elizabeth Peabody (the sister of his wife Sophia, who championed the entrance of women into fields to which they had been denied access), and Mary Peabody Mann (another Peabody sister, the wife of Horace Mann, founder and first President of Antioch College, the first college in the country to admit women as students).[2] Through these relatives, friends, and acquaintances, Hawthorne became aware of the most sophisticated feminist thought of his day, and the grinding groundbreaking daily efforts that women were making to enter the public sphere to which they had been denied access or to which they had lost access.

In *Sexual Politics*, Kate Millett has observed the profound contradiction between prevailing nineteenth-century myths which idealized women and perceived them to be the repositories of goodness and virtue, and the reality of women's lives. The myth held that 'woman was superbly well cared for by [man,] her "natural protector"'(66). Yet, under common law, women

> underwent 'civil death' upon marriage, forfeiting what amounted to every human right . . . . Her husband owned both her person and her services . . . . All that the wife acquired by her labor . . . became the legal property of the male . . . . Should the husband die intestate, the state might pick over his property (for all property was legally his) leaving the widow nothing at all, or as little as it chose to bestow upon her. (66–7)

Hawthorne had experienced in his own life the consequences of the legal system which left widows and their children in a state of penury. His father, a seaman, had died of yellow fever in early March 1808, when Nathaniel was four years old, 'intestate with little to leave his family—that little reduced by the medical and burial expenses'.[3] After all the bills were paid, there was but $296.21 remaining.[4] His mother, Elizabeth Clarke Manning Ha(w)thorne, was forced to move back into her father's house, and she spent the rest of her life in the seclusion that society insisted upon for widows, and dependent upon the whims and financial generosity of her brother Richard Manning.

Hawthorne himself, far from fulfilling his society's definition of a man who provides for the physical needs of his family, did not, for many years, earn enough money to marry his fiancée, Sophia Peabody, and, after their marriage, to support her and their first child, Una.[5] They were so poor that they barely had enough food to eat, and could not afford to rent their own home. Reading Hawthorne's fictional portraits of women against his mother's and his wife's lives permits the feminist critic to explore if Hawthorne, the writer, honestly depicted the harsh economic realities of women's lives in the nineteenth century in his fiction, or if he too participated in the patriarchal mythmaking of his time by misrepresenting women in his novels as romanticized or idealized portraits.

Again and again in writing his fiction, Hawthorne turned to a period in American history which is extremely important to feminist critics, to the 'early history of his native New England',[6] and, especially, to the period of the Salem witchcraft trials, in which his own ancestor, John Hathorne, had been a judge who had condemned a number of women accused of witchcraft to death. According to family legend, with which Hawthorne was well acquainted, one of the judge's victims pronounced a curse upon him and upon his descendants: 'God will give you blood to drink!'[7] which Hawthorne incorporated into the structure of his novel, *The House of the Seven Gables*. John Hathorne was the son of William Hathorne, 'the most dreaded magistrate in the Bay Colony', whose zeal for 'promoting moral rectitude' was accomplished by using the tortures which were legally available to him: 'burning, maiming, branding, and hanging'. Two hundred years later, 'Nathaniel Hawthorne studied the accounts of his first American ancestor with fascination and horror'.[8] And he incorporated that figure into the 'The Custom-House' of *The Scarlet Letter*:

> The figure of that first ancestor, invested by family tradition with a dim and dusky grandeur, was present to my boyish imagination, as far back as I can remember. It still haunts me, ... this grave, bearded, sable-cloaked, and steeple-crowned progenitor,—who came so early, with his Bible and his sword. ... He had all the Puritanic traits, both good and evil. (9)

The stories, sketches, and novels (among them, 'Alice Doane's Appeal', Endicott and the Red Cross', 'Main Street', 'Young Goodman Brown', 'The Maypole of Merry Mount', *The Scarlet Letter, The House of the Seven Gables)* which present Hawthorne's nineteenth-century analysis of 'the suppression of dissidents, the banishment of Anglicans, the slaughter of Indians, and the hanging of Quakers and witches'[9] unleashed by seventeenth-century Puritanism, is a body of literature which no feminist critic or historian can afford to ignore, not only because of the record which it presents of this important period in American history, but also because it records how a man like Hawthorne responded to ancestors who epitomize everything that feminist historians have identified as the characteristics of a patriarchy: repression, intolerance, sadism, tyranny, misogyny.[10]

Hawthorne's work provides us with a number of portraits of women which he either directly or indirectly associated with the feminist cause—Hester Prynne in *The Scarlet Letter*, Zenobia in *The Blithedale Romance*, and Sibyl Dacy in *Septimus Felton*. As Neal Frank Doubleday has observed, Hawthorne *never* supports the feminist efforts of these characters, but rather always criticizes them, for, although he may sympathize with the hopes of these women for a better world, 'Hawthorne's position is plain: there is no abstract solution for a problem so complicated by the nature of humanity itself'.[11]

To Doubleday, Hester Prynne, the central character in *The Scarlet Letter*, outcast in Puritan society by virtue of her adulterous relationship with a man whom she refuses to name, is 'a type feminist' (826). And David Leverenz has argued that Hester's feminism is 'radical' for she imagines a world in which gender-determined behaviour will no longer exist (558). But, 'Hester, in her distress, falls into errors that are like opinions Hawthorne saw as errors in his own time',[12] and chapter XIII is a discourse upon what Hawthorne perceives as the fundamental logical fallacy of any feminist movement:

> She discerns, it may be, such a hopeless task before her. As a first step, the whole system of society is to be torn down, and built up anew. Then, the very nature of the opposite sex, or its long hereditary habit, which has become like nature, is to be essentially modified, before woman can be allowed to assume what seems a fair and suitable position. (165)

Doubleday argues that Hawthorne sees the feminist cause as hopeless because although it might be possible to rebuild the structure of society, feminists would have to take upon themselves the even more impossible task of changing, not merely the *behaviour* of men, but the essential 'nature of the opposite sex', or habitual behaviour, so long-lived, that it might as well be considered 'like nature'. Hawthorne argues that feminist reform is impossible because it glosses the fact that gender determines behaviour.

For Hawthorne, woman's truest life is lived, not *in* the world, but on some other, more spiritual plane. Thus real problems, like want of food, shelter, and clothing, need not concern her if she is a true woman, for it is 'the ethereal essence, wherein she has her truest life' (165–6). Like Patmore's later image of the woman as 'angel in the house', Hawthorne too really believed that women were ethereal angelic substances.[13] The feminist movement, which postulated women as substantial beings with bodies, could make little sense in his cosmology. And Hawthorne believed that when a woman found herself in difficulty, she alone, and not society, was responsible for her destitution, because she had abandoned her natural womanhood. Any difficulty that a woman encounters is perceived as being caused by her deviance from her natural womanly role, and Hawthorne expounded this view in novel after novel, tale after tale. As he phrases it in *The Scarlet Letter*:

> A woman never overcomes these problems by any exercise of thought. They are not to be solved, or only in one way. If her heart chance to come uppermost, they vanish. Thus, Hester Prynne, whose heart had lost its regular and healthy throb, wandered without a clew in the dark labyrinth of mind; now turned aside by an insurmountable precipice; now starting back from a deep chasm. There was wild and ghastly scenery all around her, and a home and comfort nowhere. (166)

A passage in *Blithedale* summarizes Hawthorne's belief that a woman's feminism is always linked to her failure at love:

> women, however intellectually superior, so seldom disquiet themselves about the rights or wrongs of their sex, unless their own individual affections chance to lie in idleness, or to be ill at ease. They are not natural reformers, but become such by the pressure of exceptional misfortune.

Zenobia's reformist efforts in this novel become nothing more significant than a response to her not having been able to fulfil her 'natural' feminine role which is to love a man.

Hawthorne clearly compares the fate he plots for Hester in *The Scarlet Letter*, not only to the feminist reformers of his own time, but also to earlier women reformers, like Anne Hutchinson, with whom Hester is compared.[14] Hawthorne's criticism of Hester's behaviour suggests not only that women cannot accomplish *feminist* reform, but also that women, by their very nature, cannot ever hope to accomplish reforms of *any* sort.

Moreover, not only is it impossible for reformist women to change men's nature sufficiently to accomplish *any* meaningful social reform, but in addition women, by their very nature, cannot be helped. In one of his last works, *Septimus Felton*, Sibyl Dacy speculates about what she will do 'for women in the aeons of existence Septimus promises her'. And she concludes: 'if it turns out—as I suspect—that woman is not capable of being helped, that there is something inherent in herself that makes it hopeless to struggle for her redemption, then what shall I do?'[15] Any attempt at change is therefore futile. Even if man were to change his nature, even if social institutions were to change, the feminist reform movement would ultimately founder because of woman's nature, which 'is not capable of being helped': in Hawthorne's world there is no reason to ever attempt change of *any* kind: things are as they must be because women and men are as they always have been and will always be.

Hawthorne's biographical sketch of Anne Hutchinson, titled 'Mrs Hutchinson', which appeared in the *Salem Gazette* in 1830, is an extremely important document for examining his beliefs about feminism and women.[16]

Hawthorne is not interested in recounting for his audience the considerable heroic accomplishments of this liberal religious woman, who was one of the founders of Rhode Island; who organized women to explore their own views of theology; who promulgated the idea that intuition, and not organized, institutionalized religion was the method of choice in attaining salvation; who fought Puritanism for its repressive and tyrannical theocracy; and who was banished from Massachusetts Bay Colony. Rather, Hutchinson, for Hawthorne, is, quite simply, the kind of woman who poses a threat to society and whom society *must* expel. Moreover, he argues,

> there are portentous indications, changes gradually taking place in the habits and feelings of the gentle sex, which seem to threaten our posterity with many of those public women, whereof one [Hutchinson] was a burden too grievous for our fathers. (1)

Hawthorne states that because there were more public women in his own day than in Hutchinson's, public women pose an even greater threat to men in his own time than Hutchinson did in hers, simply because she acted singly.

Hawthorne observes that the 'medium through which feminine ambition chiefly manifests itself' in his own day is through literature, so that the literary women of his time are as threatening as Hutchinson: 'The hastiest glance may show how much of the texture and body of . . . literature is the work of those slender fingers from which only a light and fanciful embroidery has heretofore been required . . .' (1–2). But this is not as it should be; this is a perversion of the natural order. Women, by their very nature, were never meant to be writers. For a woman to write is 'an irregularity' (3). Moreover, to be a writer, one must possess an intellect, and women simply do not possess this necessary component of any writer's equipment:

> Women's intellect should never give the tone to that of man; and even her morality is not exactly the material for masculine virtue. A false liberality, which mistakes the strong division

> lines of Nature for arbitrary distinctions, ... [has added] a girlish feebleness to the tottering infancy of our literature. (2)

This entrance of women into the literary realm, however, is not merely unfortunate: it is an 'evil [which] is likely to be a growing one' (2); and even though women shouldn't be able to write because they do not have the brains to be able to do it, none the less, Hawthorne paradoxically sees writing women as a threat that is so great that literary women are 'ink-stained Amazons' who 'will expel their [male] rivals by actual pressure, and petticoats [will] wave triumphantly over all the field' (2).

But Hawthorne then poses the question of whether or not fame, when won by a woman, is a 'prize worth having' (3). And he argues, quite simply, that it is not, primarily because when women have fame, they do not necessarily gain an even greater prize, the respect of men. Hawthorne argues that certain men (and he is one of them) perceive 'a sort of impropriety in the display of woman's natal mind to the gaze of the world' (3). When a woman 'feels the impulse of genius', Hawthorne urges her to understand that 'she is relinquishing a part of the loveliness of her sex' and if she obeys her 'inward voice' which urges her to create, she should obey it, not with joy at her capacity, but, instead, 'with sorrowing reluctance' (3). In later years, Hawthorne reiterated his views on women authors when he wrote to his publisher 'All women, as author's [*sic*], are feeble and tiresome. I wish they were forbidden to write, on pain of having their faces deeply scarified with an oyster shell.'[17]

When Hawthorne ends his digression on women novelists (which, of course, is no digression at all), and gets back to Anne Hutchinson, it becomes clear that he views her just as he views women writers: as a deviant. In her native land, she had '*shown symptoms of irregular* ... thought' (3); she 'could *find no peace in this chosen land*'; she began to 'promulgate *strange and dangerous* opinions' (3) which '*eat into its* [the Colony's] *very existence*' (4), she is '*the disturber of Israel* (8).[18]

When he describes her trial, his narrative is extremely vivid:

> A crowd of hooded women, and of men in steeple-hats and close-cropped hair, are assembled at the door. ... An earnest expression glows in every face. ... We, also, will go in, edging through the thronged doorway. ... At the upper end, behind a table, on which are placed the Scriptures and two glimmering lamps, we see a woman ... (4–5)

His rhetorical strategy forces the reader to share the role of those who persecute her. He argues that the Colony was fully justified in its persecution: hers was 'a most remarkable case in which religious freedom was wholly inconsistent with public safety' (7). Thus, he aligns himself with his own Hathorne ancestors who were so diligent in seeking out heresy and in crushing it, and Hawthorne's treatment of Anne Hutchinson in print is the equivalent of his ancestor William Hathorne's colleagues' treatment of her in reality.[19]

The leaders who persecute her are 'those blessed fathers of the land, who rank in our veneration next to the evangelists of Holy Writ'; those who follow her teachings are 'unpurified from the fiercest errors of the age, ... ready to propagate the religion of peace by violence' (9). And Hutchinson herself

> stands loftily before her judges with a determined brow; and unknown to herself, there is a flash of carnal pride half hidden in her eyes, as she surveys the many learned and famous men whom her doctrines have put in fear. (10)

This description is a cheap shot: it degrades Anne Hutchinson and it perverts her religious mission by rendering her as little more than an arrogant man-hating whore in religious reformer's clothing, totally unaware of the fact that her religious zeal is founded in her own unadmitted and unexamined lust.

Not only is Hutchinson banished, Providence sees fit to punish her with the worst punishment that a woman can endure:

> she lost her husband, who is mentioned in history only as attending her footsteps, and whom we may conclude to have

> been (like most husbands of celebrated women) a mere insignificant appendage of his mightier wife. (11)

Although it is often held, in critical circles, that Nathaniel Hawthorne was opposed to the repressive policies of his own Puritan forebears,[20] a careful reading of 'Mrs Hutchinson' forces one to conclude that he was as unsympathetic to her attempt at reforming the tyrannical excesses of the Puritan theocracy as he was to the feminist cause in the nineteenth century.

For nineteenth-century feminists, Hutchinson's most significant teaching was 'the exercise of individual rights, by either sex or by any group' in matters of theology: 'If God, not the ordained clergy, picks His spokesmen, then women are as likely as any to be among the chosen.'[21] If, as Hutchinson argued, women were equal to men before God, it would be difficult, if not impossible, to maintain that they were not equal to men on earth.

Hawthorne's essay must be read as an oblique censuring of the nineteenth-century feminist movement because in Transcendental circles Hutchinson was considered to be 'the first Transcendentalist and, by extension, the first feminist in America'.[22] Any criticism of Hutchinson made by Hawthorne, therefore, would be applied to the contemporary feminists of his time as well.

Hawthorne was no more generous in his assessment of the feminist Margaret Fuller, his contemporary, than he was in his treatment of Anne Hutchinson. In fact, many of his remarks about Fuller and the feminists of his own time are strikingly similar to his remarks about Hutchinson.[23]

Through Fuller's *Woman in the Nineteenth Century*, Hawthorne had read the view expressed that women's behaviour was not 'the order of nature' (115) and could be changed, as well as her challenge for woman 'to lay aside all thought, such as she habitually cherishes, of being taught and led by men' (119). These were radical challenges in a century that believed that women's piety, purity, submissiveness and domesticity',[24] the four cardinal virtues of women's behaviour, were grounded in her innate female nature and not in what she had been trained to be. He had also come to know Fuller's belief that being a slave and being a woman were identical conditions. Perhaps Sophia Hawthorne expressed her husband's views as well as her own when, after the publication of Fuller's work, she wrote to her mother:

> It seems to me that if she were married truly, she would no longer be puzzled about the rights of woman. This is the revelation of woman's true destiny and place, which never can be *imagined* by those who do not experience the relation. . . . Had there never been false and profane marriages, there would not only be no commotion about woman's rights, but it would be Heaven here at once . . . I do not believe any man who ever knew one noble woman would ever speak as if she were an inferior in any sense: it is the fault of ignoble women that there is any such opinion in the world.[25]

Even though Hawthorne himself censured Fuller in her lifetime for her views, after her death, when he found out about the illegitimacy of her child, he was even more brutal. He wrote:

> It was such an awful joke, that she should have resolved—in all sincerity, no doubt,—to make herself the greatest, wisest, best woman of the age. And to that end she set to work on her strong, heavy, unpliable, and in many respects defective and evil nature.

He remarked upon how she 'fell as the weakest of her sisters might' and he forgave her, concluding 'I do not know that I like her better for it; because she proved herself a very woman after all'. The arrogant and persecutory nature of his tone cannot be dismissed.

Hawthorne believed that Fuller *deserved* to die as she did—she, her husband, and child died by drowning when their ship foundered just off the shore of Fire Island—because Fuller had overstepped her bounds as a woman, and because he had ascertained that her nature was evil:

> Thus there appears to have been a total collapse in poor Margaret, morally and intellectually; and tragic as her catastrophe was, Providence was, after all, kind in putting her and her clownish husband and their child aboard that fated ship.[26]

The views Hawthorne held about the nature of women and men reflected the most conservative of the prevailing stereotypes of his time rather than the feminist challenge to those stereotypes, as his statements about Hutchinson and Fuller indicate. Like others of his time, Hawthorne believed in the

> differences between the sexes and that these differences were total and innate. Women were inherently more religious, modest, passive, submissive and domestic than men, and were happier doing tasks, learning lessons, and playing games that harmonized with their nature.[27]

As Hawthorne himself claimed, any deviation from these prescribed roles would result in the total collapse of the order of society, because the order of society was based upon absolute knowledge of the innate and therefore absolute differences between women and men. The role of woman in this cosmology was rigidly defined: she was 'Earth-Mother, whose life-giving body and powers were beyond the power of mere man'; her 'cerebral system [was] less well-developed' than man's, and so she was unsuited to cerebral tasks—woman was, therefore, the reactor, man, the thinker, the doer, and if she deviated from her assigned place, 'she deserved everything she got: a short unhappy life, dementia, death and a total lack of respect from men or virtuous women'.[28]

And yet, Hawthorne's exploration of the sexual life of characters like Hester, Zenobia, and Miriam, reticent though they may appear, can be read in the context of the loosening attitudes towards the discussion of female sexuality that was taking place in the United States. According to Ann Snitow, before the 1870s 'the topic of female sexual experience was largely taboo in public and private discussion' although feminists in the 1830s and 1840s had made the equation between the ways in which men expressed their sexuality and the oppression of women. The end of the century saw 'a new frankness' in 'feminist sexual discussion' that turned upon 'social purity . . . and voluntary motherhood'. Feminists created 'an abstract image of woman as sexual victim' as a strategy for urging social reform, which, unfortunately, 'became a weapon with which the male ruling class . . . strengthened its hegemony over women . . .' (21–2).

Hawthorne's portraits of women are illuminated when read in this context, for, in virtually all of his novels, opposed as he was to feminism, there are portraits of women as sexual victims, a definition of women that was identical to that described by the feminists of his time.

Joyce W. Warren has asserted that although Hawthorne was able to portray 'real flesh-and-blood women . . . who cannot be downstaged by assertive male superpersons', his 'strong women are never allowed to pursue what might seem to be the implications of their characters; they do not become heroic leaders or independent public figures'. For Warren, 'this hesitation is owing in part to Hawthorne's belief in a conventional image of feminine behavior' (189).

None of Hawthorne's strong women characters who deviate from their culture's norms meets a happy end in his novels. In this regard, therefore, Hawthorne's novels can be seen in the tradition of those women novelists of his time who praised 'the virtues of submissiveness, piety, purity, and domesticity', making 'it clear that a woman was judged according to how well she lived up to this ideal'.[29] Hawthorne's Hester, Zenobia, and Miriam all meet tragic or unhappy ends. Their fate might appear, on the surface, to be radically different from that of women in women's novels of the time (and from Ellen's fate in *Fanshawe*). Women's novels generally conclude with successful marriages, indicating that the heroine has resolved the basic dilemma of the novel—'the formation and assertion of a feminine ego'[30] as defined by her society. Nevertheless, Hawthorne's novels and the nineteenth-century women's tradition are identical in their underlying 'certainty that men and women were essentially different. . . . [T]hey saw this distinction as significant enough to warrant a stratified society based on it, with appropriately different behavior and occupations for the two sexes.'[31] Reading Hawthorne's work within the context of a woman's tradition which reached the peak of its success by the end of the 1850s, and which included within its ranks women novelists like Catherine Maria Sedgwick and Caroline Lee Hintz,[32] provides the feminist critic with an opportunity to explore the impact of the women's tradition upon a male writer, an influence that is customarily ignored.

The only novel in the nineteenth century which totally escaped the century's stereotypic view of women, the only novel which seriously challenged and subverted 'the exclusiveness of the myth of American male individualism' and 'the traditional role of women' was not one of Hawthorne's novels, but, rather, Fanny Fern's *Ruth Hall* (1855), which portrays 'a female protagonist who succeeds wholly on her own', who does not marry, who 'becomes rich and successful through hard work and her own talents—without the help of and in spite of the cruelty of the men in the novel'.[33]

Oddly enough, although the language he uses to praise its author suggests that a good woman writer is in league with the devil, Hawthorne himself liked *Ruth Hall*:

> The woman writes as if the devil was in her; and that is the only condition under which a woman ever writes anything worth reading. . . . [W]hen they throw off the restraints of decency, and come before the public stark naked, as it were—then their books are sure to possess character and value.[34]

There are no Ruth Halls in Hawthorne's fiction, although Hawthorne himself knew women who, like Ruth Hall, lived extraordinarily productive lives without marrying or succumbing to the limitations imposed by their sex.

One of these women was Elizabeth Palmer Peabody, sister of his wife Sophia, who must be numbered among the most accomplished women of her own—or indeed, of any—

generation. Influenced by Madame de Stael, Elizabeth Palmer Peabody believed that 'genius has no sex', that a 'Golden Age was dawning', and that she would 'play an important part'[35] in it. Family tradition held that 'the Peabody clan were descendants of Boadicea, Queen of the Britons',[36] and Elizabeth surely acted as if she believed it.

Louise Hall Tharp's *The Peabody Sisters of Salem* and Ruth M. Baylor's *Elizabeth Palmer Peabody: Kindergarten Pioneer* are among the works which document Elizabeth's numerous and extraordinary accomplishments: she was 'a serious scholar of theology and history';[37] she was the author of no less than twenty-seven books (such as *First Steps to the Study of History*; *Part II: The Hebrews; Part III, The Greeks*);[38] and 125 articles, on topics such as theology and sociology ('The Being of God', 'Ego-theism, the Atheism of Today', 'Social Crime and Its Retribution'), the kindergarten movement and childhood education ('Order of Development in Children', 'Phenomena of Child Life', 'The Origin of the Kindergarten') and the education of women ('Industrial Schools for Women', 'Female Education in Massachusetts'). She edited many other works, such as, *Aesthetic Papers* and *Crimes of the House of Austria Against Mankind,* through which she brought to the attention of the American people the plight of the Hungarians.[39] She was the first woman lecturer in the United States, whose series, 'Historical School', originated in her 'own disappointment that women were denied access to higher education' and was the forerunner of Margaret Fuller's 'Conversations'; she was the first woman to teach boys, and the first woman to do evening lecturing, thus breaking the gender barrier in both these fields; she recorded Bronson Alcott's conversations with children at Temple School in *Record of a School Exemplifying the Principles and Methods of Moral Culture* and she promoted his method; she advanced the cause of mesmerism by translating from the French an article about Mesmer, 'and she felt sure that she herself had "magnetism"'. She brought together the leading thinkers of her day by, for example, introducing Alcott to Ralph Waldo Emerson. She was the first woman publisher in Boston, her first publication being William Ellery Channing's *Emancipation* (1840), which advanced the cause of the Antislavery Society. In addition, she published the *Dial* and Hawthorne's *Grandfather's Chair*, *Famous Old People* and *Liberty Tree*.

Her work actively advanced such radical causes as a universal language, emancipation for slaves, the Brook Farm experiment, the teaching of music, dancing, art, and physical fitness. She was the founder of the kindergarten in America, and she 'established the first public kindergarten in the United States'; she went to Washington several times in her life to lobby on behalf of Native Americans. In her eighties, she took on the 'cause for equal suffrage', holding Woman Suffrage meetings in her home; at ninety, she turned her attention to the cause of world peace.[40]

His sister-in-law Elizabeth was a constant source of exasperation to Hawthorne,[41] even though she was enormously helpful to him. She persuaded George Bancroft to arrange for Hawthorne to become 'Weigher and Gauger' at the Boston Custom House; she arranged meetings between him and Emerson, Longfellow, Holmes, Sarah Clarke, Margaret Fuller, and others;[42] she published his works; and it was she who had first discovered his writings in a magazine under a pen-name and who wrote to Horace Mann that Hawthorne was a 'man of first rate genius'.[43] That Elizabeth none the less represented a kind of woman who fascinated him is evident from a dream that he naively described to his wife Sophia in June 1848. In the dream, Sophia 'hadst now ceased to be my wife' and 'thy sister Elizabeth . . . informed the company that . . . having ceased to be thy husband, I of course became hers'.[44]

Hawthorne was aware, through the example of Elizabeth Peabody's life, that it was, in fact, possible for a woman to lead a public life of great accomplishment, without tragic results. None the less, he organized the rearing of his and Sophia's three children Una, Julian, and Rose, according to the most rigid gender-bound expectations of his time. And, although he encouraged Sophia to develop her talents as an artist within the context of the home, he greeted with oppression any attempt on the part of his daughters to break out of his definition of appropriate behaviour for a woman. This, despite the fact that it was the money ('a hundred and fifty dollars in bills, in silver, even in coppers') [45] which Sophia had saved from painting screens and lampshades which bought the time for him to write *The Scarlet Letter*, his masterpiece.[46]

According to Julian Hawthorne, 'the most fortunate event of his life was, probably, his marriage with Sophia Peabody'. After her marriage to Nathaniel, Sophia found a new source for strength, and she was, for the first time since her infancy, in perfect health; nor did she ever afterwards relapse into her previous condition of invalidism, in all likelihood caused by the medications she had been given as a child. After their marriage, Hawthorne encouraged her talent as an artist, and, at one point, wrote to Margaret Fuller about his wishes for Sophia:

> I wish to remove everything that might impede her full growth and development,—which in her case, it seems to me, is not to be brought about by care and toil, but by perfect repose and happiness. . . . Besides, she has many visions of great deeds to be wrought on canvas and in marble during the coming autumn and winter; and none of these can be accomplished unless she can retain quite as much freedom from household drudgery as she enjoys at present.[47]

Hawthorne and Sophia colluded in creating a mythology of their marriage in which they were the new Adam and Eve, which, according to T. Walter Herbert, was an example of a widespread nineteenth-century phenomenon, 'the sacralization of domestic intimacy'.[48] This myth seriously distorted the truth of the reality of their lives, and presented grave and almost insurmountable problems for Sophia after Hawthorne's death. Although his love letters to her describe what has been called 'a passionate, physical relationship', none the less, in letters to her during their courtship—he destroyed almost all of hers to him[49]—she is his Dove, embodying 'the Holy Spirit',[50] or 'naughty Sophie Hawthorne':[51]

> Belovedest, I love thee. But then that naughty Sophie Hawthorne—it would be out of the question to treat her with tenderness. Nothing shall she get from me . . . save a kiss upon her nose; and I should not wonder if she were to return the favor with a buffet upon my ear. Mine own Dove, how unhappy art thou to be linked with such a mate! . . .—and me unhappy, too, to be forced to keep such a turbulent little rebel in my inmost heart.[52]

Repeatedly, throughout his love letters, Hawthorne describes his feelings of unworthiness in the face of her divine goodness: 'I suppose I should have pretty much the same feeling if an angel were to come from Heaven and be my dearest friend.'[53] And he describes his terror of losing her, should she decide to follow the dictates of her nature and desert him by becoming mere spirit. (Hawthorne had written a poem at sixteen about 'a young man dying for love of a ghost.')[54]

Because she is an angel, she is expected to forgive him, and she is expected, as well, not to suffer if he wrongs her: 'Oh, let me feel that I may even do you a little wrong without your avenging it (oh how cruelly) by being wounded.' After their marriage, he was the husband to whom she would willingly submit: 'my Dove is to follow my guidance and do my bidding. . . . My love gives me the right, and your love consents to it.'[55]

Thus, Sophia and Nathaniel Hawthorne lived out in their own lives that great paradox upon which the institution of marriage was based in the nineteenth century: Hawthorne, like other husbands of his time, truly believed that his wife Sophia was morally and spiritually his superior; and yet he believed that his role as head of the household provided him with the power to control her, a belief that was supported by law. Hawthorne, to his credit, considering the traditions of his time, often took on the tasks of housekeeper, to spare his wife the effort. In a 27 December 1843 letter to her mother, Sophia described how Hawthorne 'rose . . . in the mornings, and kindled fires, and by the time I come down, the tea-kettle boild, and potatoes were baked and rice cooked'. After Una's birth, Hawthorne was an enormous help to Sophia: 'My husband relieves me with her constantly, and gets her to sleep beautifully', and, for a year following her birth, according to his wife, he did not have 'a chance for one hour's uninterrupted musing, and without his desk being once opened!'[56] This was certainly remarkable behaviour for a man in Hawthorne's time, when the home and household tasks fell within the purview of woman's work.[57] The Hawthornes in their own home confronted what has become an important issue for contemporary feminists, and, in sharing the burden of childcare and housework with Sophia, Hawthorne was surely ahead of his time. The diary he kept when he spent twenty days during the summer of 1851, caring for Julian, attests to how well he understood women's work:

> I hardly know how we got through the forenoon. It is impossible to write, read, think, or even sleep (in the daytime), so constant are his appeals in one way or another; still he is such a genial and good-humored little man that there is certainly an enjoyment intermixed with all the annoyance.[58]

However, according to his son, Julian, Hawthorne was 'always very chary of his daughters'[59] and he did not believe in sending them to school. Sophia went along with him, even though Sophia had been affronted in her youth by the 'fact that only her brothers had a right to a college education'. At one time, when their daughter, Rose, was about ten years old, she was 'caught by her father in the act of writing a story and had been severely scolded and told never to do such a thing again'. Hawthorne had once written to Sophia that he was glad she had never wanted to become a writer, for a woman writer 'prostituted' herself and writing, for a woman, was akin to walking 'abroad through the streets, physically stark naked'.[60]

In 1859, Elizabeth Peabody wrote the Hawthornes, who were living in England, a vivid description of the horrors that had resulted from the Fugitive Slave Laws, telling 'the story of a young colored girl, born free but captured and exposed for sale in the deep South, naked upon the block.

She told it well, especially for Una.'[61] Not only did Hawthorne not show Elizabeth's letter to Una, he took the opportunity of instructing Elizabeth in his views about the upbringing of young women. He replied that it was impossible for him to show the letter to Una:

> I must guard Una from the ups and downs of sentiment and passion on her judgment and experience as long as I can .... She *never* reads newspapers .... I wish the 'summer calm of golden charity' to reign on Una's 'sweet lips' during this blooming into Womanhood and tender spring green of judgment. And you would display before her great, innocent eyes a naked slave girl on a block at auction (which I am sure is an exaggeration for I have read of those auctions often and even the worst facts are never so bad as absolute nudity).[62]

In Hawthorne's view, not only was Una to be kept innocent of the events in the world, Elizabeth's description of the slave girl's nudity becomes a far greater evil than the fact of slavery itself.

T. Walter Herbert has argued that Una's harsh and repressive upbringing resulted in her bouts of insanity, which were treated by 'an early form of electroshock therapy'. Herbert describes entries in Hawthorne's diaries which document Una's attempts to depart from her father's belief 'that the subordination of women to men was in conformity with the laws of Nature and of Nature's God'; '[Una] resists—father insists—there is a terrible struggle—and she gets into almost a frenzy.'[63]

Yet because of her upbringing, Una had herself internalized Hawthorne's belief that the ultimate role for woman was passive submission to the will of a man, and she interpreted her own wish to rebel from these restrictions as Hawthorne did, as evidence that there was something profoundly evil within her. As Hawthorne himself phrased it: '... I now and then catch an aspect of her, in which I cannot believe her to be my own human child, but a spirit strangely mingled with good and evil, haunting the house where I dwell'; and, as Una echoed:

> Though I appear, & am, perfectly well while I do as I please, (did you ever know such a wilful & headstrong young woman as I am?) there is a certain little group of events & sights & minds that in a minute by a most wonderful magic make me faint & sick & all over shooting pains.[64]

For Herbert, Hawthorne's character Pearl in *The Scarlet Letter* is a fictional transcription of his belief that his daughter's nature was fundamentally evil. Herbert describes the case of Una Hawthorne, too, as an example, *par excellence*, of 'the collective response of middle-class Northeastern women in the 19th century . . . whose lives predominantly featured dramas of thwarted strength'.[65]

The supreme irony of Hawthorne's life and his disapproval of the feminist movement, and his insistence on 'ladylike' behaviour for his wife and daughters, was that, after his death, his wife and children suffered the consequences. For, repeating the history of his father, Hawthorne left his family in dire financial circumstances. Not once, during his lifetime, had he asked his publisher to present him with an accounting, or the sum owed him, which he never collected during his lifetime, and after his death none of Sophia's inquiries about the balance she believed she was owed was answered.

Even worse than not providing for them, however, was the fact that he left his wife with a set of principles about womankind that prohibited her from helping herself and her children. When Una, facing the fact that she would have to provide for her own well-being, told her mother that she wanted to earn her own living as a physical education teacher, and that 'a class of ladies had been promised', her mother took to her bed. When a clergyman stated that he approved of woman suffrage, Sophia told Una that it was her obligation to remind him that it was 'men for the rostrum, women for the home', and that this was 'the will of God', even though no one would provide for Una if she remained at home. When Sophia was asked to write Hawthorne's biography, in part to ease her desperate financial situation, she refused, remembering Hawthorne's opinion of women writers, despite the fact that her own sister, Mary, had written Horace Mann's biography.[66]

Hawthorne's novels, and the example of his life are invaluable for feminist inquiry. Because Hawthorne himself was fully aware of the struggle for women's rights, the feminist critic is provided with an opportunity to explore how one American male writer, regarded as among the country's finest, reacted, in his works and in his life, to the feminist movement. Whatever else they may be, Hawthorne's novels can be read as an uneasy masculine exploration of, and reaction to, the radical, revolutionary claims that the feminists of his time were making about the nature of women, and the solutions to the reality of their abject outsider economic, political, and legal status within the American system.

CHAPTER TWO

Feminists and Nathaniel Hawthorne

In 1970, Kate Millett's *Sexual Politics* defined a feminist stance towards works of fiction written by men in patriarchal societies that was as shocking as it was perceptive and useful. Millett argued that these works of fiction should not be regarded as artistic artifacts that exist in a vacuum, as any 'art for art's sake' definition holds. Nor should the novelist necessarily be regarded as a humanist, filled with reverence and good will towards women and men. Male novelists, she observed, are not immune from misogyny, one of the governing principles of a patriarchy.

Moreover, (and more importantly), Millett stated that works of literature are one of society's most powerful vehicles for expressing and promulgating male dominance over women: 'Of all artistic forms in patriarchy it is the most frankly propagandistic. Its aim is to reinforce both sexual factions in their status' (45).

In close readings of excerpts from the novels of writers such as Henry Miller and Norman Mailer, Millett demonstrated how fictive portraits of male/female relationships very often encode and justify brutally sadistic treatment towards female characters who do not comply with the social norm of male ascendancy in matters of sexuality and/or power. The message to women in these works is abundantly clear: 'Females who are . . . not sexually compliant, should be beaten' (9). The message to men is also clear: being male means having the gender-determined right to dominate a woman and to enforce that dominance by any means, including physical violence. Millett also argued that 'two leading myths of Western culture' often underpin descriptions of women's behaviour in novels: 'the classical tale of Pandora's box and the Biblical story of the Fall' and that these myths are 'influential ethical justifications of things as they are' (51).

Millett's work provided a mode of inquiry for feminist literary critics. It alerted them to the misogynist attitudes in literature that previously had been ignored. Her work prompted a flurry of critical inquiry into male texts that, as of this writing, shows no signs of abating. Although she did not refer specifically to the work of Nathaniel Hawthorne, Millett none the less provided a method for exploring whether or not misogynist attitudes were expressed in Hawthorne's novels.

Feminist critics of Hawthorne differ dramatically on the issue of whether or not Hawthorne shared the misogynist attitudes of his time, or whether he criticized them. Carolyn G. Heilbrun in *Toward a Recognition of Androgyny* has read *The Scarlet Letter* as a singular novel in the American experience, one which does not turn its back 'on the "feminine impulse"', in which the portrait of Hester Prynne 'is never chiseled down to fit a conventional view of women's limitations': ' ... America has not produced a novel whose androgynous implications match those of *The Scarlet Letter*, nor a novel with as great a central female character' (63). Other critics have maintained that, although Hawthorne may present portraits of extraordinarily powerful women in his fiction, his narrative stance towards those women is one of extreme ambivalence, if not outright hostility. As David Leverenz has stated of *The Scarlet Letter* in 'Mrs Hawthorne's headache':

> What starts as a feminist revolt against punitive patriarchal society ends in a muddle of sympathetic pity for ambiguous victims. Throughout, a gentlemanly moralist frames the story so curiously as to ally his empathies with his inquisitions. (553)

Feminist critics of Nathaniel Hawthorne employ a number of critical approaches to arrive at their conclusions, and the very finest critics employ an eclectic approach which, for example, might combine close-reading techniques, psychoanalytic inquiry, as well as methodologies derived from historiography and social science. It is, therefore, impossible to sort Hawthorne feminist criticism into any neat category system. None the less, the directions which recent feminist inquiry have taken can be summarized as follows: 1) criticism which (following the lead of Millett) explores the misogynist implications of Hawthorne's works by using close-reading techniques or analysing the structure of the works, such as the 'resisting reader' technique developed by Judith Fetterley; 2) criticism which examines Hawthorne's work in the context of how other male writers were depicting female characters, as in the work of Judith Fryer, Wendy Martin and Joyce W Warren; 3) criticism which examines Hawthorne's treatment of women in his life and in his art, as in the work of T. Walter Herbert, Nina Baym, Gloria C. Erlich, and Joyce W. Warren; 4) criticism which reads Hawthorne's work as a demonstration of women's power, as in the work of Nina Auerbach, Nina Baym, Carolyn Heilbrun, and Joyce W. Warren; 5) criticism which explores Hawthorne's portraits of women within the context of the prevailing mythology of his times, as in the work of Judith Fryer, Sandra Gilbert and Susan Gubar, T. Walter Herbert, and Joyce W. Warren; 6) criticism which analyses the impact of the women in Hawthorne's life upon his work, or reads his novels in the context of the women's tradition in literature, as in the work of Nina Baym, Gloria C. Erlich, T. Walter Herbert, and Joyce W. Warren.

Judith Fetterley's *The Resisting Reader* explores the political implications of the fact that the American literary tradition is male. Fetterley poses a critical question based on reader-response theory: what happens to a woman when she reads a novel whose value system is predominantly male and often misogynist? According to Fetterley, 'women are taught to think as men, to identify with a male point of view, and to accept as normal and legitimate a male system of values, one of whose central principles is misogyny' (xx).

As a response to this fact, a woman must 'become a resisting rather than an assenting reader, . . . to begin the process of exorcizing the male mind that has been implanted in us' (xxii).

Fetterley develops a feminist reading of central texts in American literature, among them Nathaniel Hawthorne's 'The Birthmark'. In the tale, Aylmer, a scientist, wants his beautiful wife Georgiana to be physically perfect and so he persuades her to allow him to remove a birthmark. But although the birthmark disappears, Georgiana dies. Fetterley states that 'The Birthmark' demonstrates a recurring theme in American literature: 'the drama of men's power over women' which is disguised, by Hawthorne, behind 'the language of idealism' which depicts the husband's act as a striving for perfection which obscures the fact that 'Aylmer is free to experiment on Georgiana, to the point of death, because she is both woman and wife' (31). The story, then, illustrates 'the great American dream of eliminating women' and it also provides an analysis of the 'sexual politics of idealization': '"The Birthmark" demonstrates the fact that the idealization of women has its source in a profound hostility toward women and that it is at once a disguise for this hostility and the fullest expression of it' (24).

The resisting woman reader must become aware of the fact that, in the American dream, 'the only good woman is a dead woman', and the 'desire to perfect' disguises 'the need to eliminate' (24). To Fetterley, although Hawthorne is no feminist, his work is implicitly feminist for it reveals 'an implicit understanding' on Hawthorne's part 'of the consequences for women' of the psychology which accompanies powerlessness: Georgiana worships Aylmer 'for his hatred of her and for his refusal to tolerate her existence' (31–2).

Judith Fryer, in *The Faces of Eve*, cites the terror that many American men felt as a result of the feminist movement's attempt to redefine women's status in the nineteenth century: to many, 'the new woman threatened not only the American home but the very survival of the race' (15). Fryer believes that Hawthorne shared the conservative need of other male novelists of his time to portray female characters according to the stereotypes dictated by the society:

> Sometimes she is Eve before the Fall, the pure and asexual preserver of American society. Sometimes she is the mother of us all, a manipulating and possessive figure. . . . Sometimes she is the 'new woman,' saying 'No!' as the first rebel Eve did to the sphere prescribed for her by the original Patriarch. (13–14)

But she is always a variant of the Eve figure, because the major mythology underpinning the American novel—and American culture—was the image of the New World as the Garden of Eden.[1] But if Eve *was* the cause of Adam's fall, in the New World reinterpretation of the possibilities of this myth, the New World Adam must resist the New World Eve's attempts to drive him out of Paradise (6).

Thus female characters are variations on 'the faces of Eve . . . : the Temptress, the American Princess, the Great Mother, the New Woman' (24). Beatrice in Hawthorne's 'Rappaccini's Daughter', Miriam, in *The Marble Faun*, are both archetypal, beautiful temptresses, whose sexuality is enormously dangerous to the male characters whom they encounter. Although Hawthorne's portrait of Hester is more complex, reflecting his own ambivalence towards her, according to Fryer she too is portrayed as tempting 'others to her own brand of lawlessness, [and] she threatens with destruction the society in which the Dimmesdales and the Hawthornes do live and serve' (84).

In sharp contrast to the Temptress, is the American Princess, who 'represents the traditional espoused values of the community' (85). Examples of this stereotype in Hawthorne's work are Priscilla in *The Blithedale Romance* and Hilda in *The Marble Faun*, both images of '"Divine Womanhood"' (94).

Although the 'woman question' was one of the most significant issues of Hawthorne's time, according to Fryer, male novelists of the nineteenth century, 'who . . . portrayed the "new woman" in their art created not women, but caricatures' (206). Thus, 'Hawthorne's Zenobia, an early leader of the women's movement', is portrayed as a deviant by Hawthorne (208), and she 'commits suicide because of her unrequited love for an inferior man' (207).

Wendy Martin in 'Seduced and abandoned in the New World' has argued that in American fiction 'women are perceived as morally inferior creatures who, beguiled by their own passions, are destined to tragic lives if they deviate from the laws of God and man' (227). She states that the depiction of passive women in the novel 'conditions its readers to accept bourgeois economic values . . .; women are encouraged to be virtuous so that they can make a good—that is, a financially respectable—marriage' (227).[2] For Martin, the myth of women as weak reflects society's definition 'of woman as a private creature, reinforcing purity, piety, and submissiveness as the proper feminine virtues and punishing those women who fail to comply with a behavior code that is economically viable in addition to being Christian' (227).

Martin sees Hawthorne's female characters as part of this need to condition women to 'accept their inferior status' (228). In *The Scarlet Letter* Hawthorne 'reminds his readers that independent thought and emotion, that is, self-reliance, can be dangerous for women' (228) and in *The Blithedale Romance*, Coverdale, the narrator, prefers the gentle, passive Priscilla to the assertive, active Zenobia, 'echoing Hawthorne himself, who had strong antifeminist predilections' (230). Martin wonders why American novelists have

> persisted in ignoring . . . examples of strong women [in American literature, like Anne Bradstreet, Elizabeth Cady Stanton, Margaret Fuller, Frances Wright, Frances Bloomer, Amelia Earhart], reinforcing instead the image of women as forlorn, helpless creatures, who are certain to be destroyed or hopelessly embittered unless they devote themselves exclusively to their domestic lives and duties as wives and mothers. (238)[3]

Sandra Gilbert and Susan Gubar in *Madwoman in the Attic* read the creation of female fictional heroines by men in the context of metaphors which depict creativity as an exclusively male act. They state that a corollary notion of male theories of authorship is that 'the chief creature man has generated is woman' (12). Thus, throughout 'the history of Western culture, ... male-engendered female figures ... have incarnated men's ambivalence not only toward female sexuality but toward their own (male) physicality' (12). Literate women learn what they are (a creation of men) and what they are supposed to be (virtuous and subject to male authority) 'as much from literature as from "life"' (11):

> The roots of 'authority' tell us, after all, that if woman is man's property then he must have authored her, just as surely as they tell us that if he authored her she must be his property. As a creation 'penned' by man, moreover, woman has been 'penned up' or 'penned in.' As a sort of 'sentence' man has spoken, she has herself been 'sentenced': fated, jailed, for he has both 'indited' her and 'indicted' her. As a thought he has 'framed,' she has been both 'framed' (enclosed) in his texts, glyphs, graphics, and 'framed up' (found guilty, found wanting) in his cosmologies. (13)

Gilbert and Gubar read the creation of angelic women by male writers within the context of a fierce misogyny that really wants women dead, and that helps control and manipulate the behaviour of women in the real world. In their view, male literary texts do not simply reflect the society or erect a mythology; they prescribe forms of behaviour which women then emulate. And the angel/woman, to them, is 'the most pernicious image' male authors have ever imposed upon women. In life, 'the cult of the angel-woman' obliged women to '"kill" themselves ... into art objects: slim, pale, passive beings whose "charms" eerily recalled the snowy, porcelain immobility of the dead'(25); it also obliged women to surrender themselves completely to the wishes of a man, and 'it is precisely this sacrifice which dooms her both to death and to heaven. For to be selfless is not only to be noble, it is to be dead' (25).

They read Hawthorne's tale, 'The Snow Image' as an

example of this theoretical stance. In the tale, a brother and sister, Peony and Violet, create a little girl out of snow, who becomes transmuted into a real person. Their father, who refuses to believe that they have, in fact, created her themselves, worries that she will be cold because she is scantily dressed, chases her, and forces her into the house, whereupon she melts into nothingness:

> From a female point of view, . . . what is most striking about . . . these snowy maidens is that ultimately they are merely snow: enchanted and inanimate as their ancestress Snow White. . . . [T]hey are powerless in the face of the male will that rules the public, actual world to which they simply present a charming but insubstantial alternative. (618)

But because the creation of a powerless, angelic female figure also entails 'her repressed (but therefore all the more frightening) capacity for explosive rage' (26), the flip side of the image of the 'angel-woman' is the 'monster-woman'. Women who take action on their own behalf are defined as 'monstrous', 'accidents of nature, [whose] deformities are meant to repel, but in their very freakishness they possess unhealthy energies, powerful and dangerous arts' (29).

In a chapter entitled 'Milton's bogey', which is especially applicable to Hawthorne's work, Gilbert and Gubar examine how eighteenth- and nineteenth-century writers seized upon the story of the Garden of Eden and used it in their literary texts, an issue which has also been discussed by the Hawthorne scholar W. H. Shurr in 'Eve's Bower'.[4] Hawthorne's view of the fall, according to Shurr, is somewhat different from the orthodox Calvinist view, in that he sees the natural world as still pure, but man as 'the frail element' (156). Yet Hawthorne still conceives of the difference between woman's nature and man's nature in orthodox terms: he sees the new Eve's consciousness growing inward 'to questions of motherhood and children—women questions which she can't share with Adam'. And the new Adam's consciousness 'likewise grows inward, but apart from her, to speculate on the male mysteries which books are written about' (159). According to Gilbert and Gubar, the Biblical tale which blames man's fall from God's grace on women, which describes how 'Eve is humbled by becoming a slave not only to her husband, but ... to the species' (197), both explains and justifies the 'historical dispossession and degradation of the female principle' (199).

Gilbert and Gubar analyse a symbol in *The Blithedale Romance*, the spectacle of the veiled lady, who seems to vanish into thin air, as reflecting 'male dread of women' (472). And they examine how the two female characters in *Blithedale*, Priscilla and Zenobia 'embody the Madonna and the Medusa aspects of the veiled lady' (472). Yet the 'feminism of Zenobia and the clairvoyance of Priscilla are linked' (472) by Hawthorne, as they were by a number of other American writers who, in their attempt to discredit the feminist movement, pointed out the historical fact that many important feminists, like Margaret Fuller, Elizabeth Cady Stanton, Lucy Stone, and Harriet Martineau, were interested in mediumism, hypnotism, automatic writing, which were seen as 'irrational psychic phenomena' (473).

Ruth Perry in *Women, Letters, and the Novel* has argued that the creation of passive, dependent female heroines must be understood within the context of the historical development of the novel as a literary form. 'The novel', according to Perry, 'must be understood as a form of literature which developed at a time of dislocating social changes' (137) which had curtailed women's economic and political power, at a time when 'they no longer participated in the means of production of the society' (137). Thus novels both reflected and taught the new social ideal: that women 'were intended solely for the business of romantic love' (138).

Nina Auerbach, in *Woman and the Demon*, has written about the curious phenomenon, that although the 'approved model of womanhood Victorians were bred to revere' (185) was the angel-woman, none the less, there is a dominance, in the imaginative literature of the time, of 'disobedient woman' as 'heir of the ages and demonic savior of her race' (2). Auerbach concludes that the 'social restrictions that crippled women's lives' during Victorian times 'were fearful attempts to exorcise a mysterious strength' (8) and cautions us to look beyond 'facile generalizations about the squeezed, crushed, and egoless Victorian woman' (189) to how the literary mythology of the time depicts women's power. She reads Hester Prynne in *The Scarlet Letter* as the epitome of 'this defiant icon' (165), a 'feminist saint, the vehicle for "a new truth" of empowered and transfigured womanhood' (166).

Ann Douglas, in *The Feminization of American Culture* has observed that by 1830, in America, there had been a radical transformation in the rights of women and a concomitant alteration of women's position in society:

> Women lost a significant number of their legal privileges, among them the right to vote. . . . They vanished more or less entirely from a number of occupations . . . To put it simply . . . the independent woman with a mind and a life of her own slowly ceased to be considered of high value. (51)

Douglas believes that the woman's tradition in literature at this time had, as its prime purpose, the preparation of women for their twin roles of saint and shopper: 'the lady's function in a capitalist society was to appropriate and preserve both the values and the commodities which her competitive husband, father and son had little time to . . . enjoy' (60). 'A Marxist might argue persuasively that American girls were socialized to immerse themselves in novels and letters in order to make their powerlessness in masculine . . . society more certain and less painful' (61). Read in this context, the 'icon of idealized if arrested femininity' (62) in novels written both by women like Sarah Josepha Hale and by male sentimentalist novelists performed the function of socializing women to their powerless new role in capitalist America. Motherhood was praised and promoted 'as tantamount, if not superior, to her lost economic productivity' (74).

Although she does not mention Hawthorne, Douglas identifies the characteristics of the narrator in sentimental novels that precisely describes the narrative stance of a number of Hawthorne novels:

> He [the narrator] comes as near as he can to the suffering of the female while savoring the titillation involved in identifying with the male who caused it. Her weakness and isolation are in a sense his own and thus he both exploits and rejects her. (239)

This attitude was adopted because the male author 'was dependent on female suffering for his material just as he was dependent on female readers for his livelihood, but he resented and subtly tried to reverse this subjugation' (239).

Cathy Davidson in 'Mothers and daughters in the fiction of the New Republic' also reads the tradition of the virtuous woman in an historical context. She traces the response to two different waves of feminism: the first, which began soon after independence; the second, in the late nineteenth century. The first wave of feminism championed 'women's greater "independence" in both public and domestic arenas' (115), and led, among other reforms, to women's academies in New England, but the second argued for 'a somewhat more restrictive "cult of domesticity"' (116). To Davidson, this reactionary change was due to the spectacle of France falling into chaos. 'Proponents of political reform who had advocated female rights in the 1770s and 1780s quickly returned to a more conservative view of women' (116).

Yet the cult of domesticity, which elevated 'Motherhood' to an enviable status was an advance, she argues, over earlier positions which had denigrated women, which saw them as 'innately licentious, impulsive, and irrational' (116). Sentimentalized portraits of women addressed themselves to an audience of women for whom 'the proper (and improper) means by which a daughter might pass into motherhood' (118) was an issue of paramount concern. Rather than an instrument for keeping women in their place, Davidson reads the sentimental tradition as reflecting the realities of life for women in the nineteenth century, and she sees the idealization of women as a real advance over earlier portraits which stressed women's evil nature. Davidson places the figure of Hester Prynne in the tradition of novels depicting the 'fallen woman' (125), a tradition which 'was . . . so prevalent in America's first popular fiction precisely because it was so true. At a time when women had neither control over their own bodies nor the vocational skills to allow them to exist independently . . ., "seduction" was to be feared' (125).

Annette Kolodny in her Introduction to *The Blithedale Romance* reads the novel in the context of the political events which were occurring in Hawthorne's day, most particularly the movement for women's rights and against slavery, the financial crisis which led to the formation of various anti-urban, agrarian, utopian experimental communities, like Brook Farm, upon which Blithedale was patterned. But Kolodny observes that Hawthorne's intention was not to write history, but to write romance, so that the novel should not be read as a fictionalized portrait of life at Brook Farm. Rather, Kolodny sees the novel as a story of 'failed possibilities and multiple human betrayals' (xviii), and of 'failed intimacy between characters of the same sex' (xix), between Coverdale and Hollingsworth as well as between Zenobia and Priscilla.

Nina Baym's 'Nathaniel Hawthorne and his mother'[5] challenges two fundamental assumptions of traditional criticism: one, that the creation of a male text derives from a male tradition and from male influence; the other, that if a woman does exert an impact on a man's life, it is a negative one. Baym argues that because Hawthorne was deeply affected by his mother's death, and because he began to work feverishly on *The Scarlet Letter* soon after, his creation of the character of Hester Prynne is best understood within the context of the impact of his mother's life on his own. She observes that most critics accuse his mother 'of a grotesque, pernicious role in his life or, alternatively, they deny her any role at all' (2):

> Common sense suggests that a work following so immediately on the death of a mother, featuring a heroine who is a mother (and whose status as a mother is absolutely central to her situation), might very likely be inspired by that death and consist, in its autobiographical substance, of a complex memorial to that mother. (2)

Baym speculates that Hawthorne turned the facts of his mother's life into the fictive experience of Hester Prynne, who, like his mother, was 'a socially stigmatized woman abandoned to bear and rear her child alone' (9).

Baym's 'Hawthorne's women' states that, in his early works, Hawthorne was interested in exploring what happens to male protagonists when they reject the qualities associated with womankind: 'warmth, imagination, intuition, and love; . . . and mysteries of the self' (250). Throughout his life, however, this early theme changed as he became 'increasingly aware of . . . the effect *on women* of the ways in which men perceived and treated them' (251). According to Baym, although Hawthorne's interests were very different from the feminists of his time, he 'concurred with the judgment that the life of woman in society was slavery', but he was more interested in discussing 'the warping and distortion of women's minds under the unremitting pressure of . . . male myths' (251) than in exploring social issues and possible changes that could be made in the social order, largely because he 'could not summon any belief in the possibility of change or progress' (272).

Gloria C. Erlich's *Family Themes and Hawthorne's Fiction* provides an important psychobiographical investigation of Hawthorne's treatment of women and sexual relationships. She argues that the recurrent themes of maternal deprivation, parental loss, domination by strong and sinister men, and the description of women as either saintly or temptresses are all to be found in the special circumstances of Hawthorne's life. An especially important chapter is 'The inner circle: Hawthorne's women' which traces the connection between his attitude to the women in his life and his creation of female characters. According to Erlich, his fiction, 'from earliest to latest, portrays many variations of the sexually tempting but taboo dark woman. Many of these occur within a context of brother-sister incest' (93).[6]

Erlich assesses Hawthorne's relationship with his dark-haired sister Ebe as the likely source for this recurrent theme. The fact that Hawthorne knew of brother–sister incest in the history of his own predecessors, in the Manning family, and that he had read contemporary accounts of the punishment of the offenders is extremely important because Hawthorne's feelings for Ebe must have reverberated with the significance of history. In addition, Erlich suggests that Hawthorne's 'tendency to give structural importance to the shadowy, often ambiguous sexual experience of his dark women may well derive from the fact that he knew his mother only as a widow' (95–6), and this might have led to his sexual curiosity about her: 'For Hawthorne, the mother's seductive image merged with Ebe's incestuous aura, the two . . . thus combining to create a maternal figure of dangerous sensuality' (98).

T. Walter Herbert's 'Little Pearl and Hawthorne's daughter: an essay in the poetics of culture' argues that Hawthorne's creation of the character of Pearl in *The Scarlet Letter* is best understood in the context of his persecutory attitude towards his own daughter Una. Neither Pearl nor Una 'have that sensitive and yielding quality of personal sympathy that Hawthorne considered innate to feminine character' (9):

> Hawthorne's uneasiness over his daughter, and his way of portraying little Pearl, are to a degree eccentric products of his personal disposition; yet they also partake of this existential anxiety as it was being felt regarding children, and especially girl-children, in early 19th century America. (9)

Joyce W. Warren's *The American Narcissus* develops the thesis that 'most American female fictional characters are not people' (1) because women 'were not regarded as persons' in American society (3):

> Persons regarded as outside the American experience—persons who by their society's definition did not themselves qualify as individualists—were not seen as individuals. Women, blacks, Indians, and other 'others' had no place in the drama of American individualism. Like the legendary Narcissus, the American individualist focused on his own image to such an extent that he could grant little reality to others. (4)

Warren observes that the 'nineteenth century marked a significant diminishment in women's freedom' and as the qualities of 'submissiveness, piety, purity, and domesticity' (8) were written into portraits of women characters, the myth of the American male was that he was all-powerful, needing no one.

Warren believes that Hawthorne's work was significantly different from most nineteenth-century American novels in that, in three of his novels (*The Scarlet Letter*, *The Blithedale Romance*, and *The Marble Faun*) Hawthorne 'was able to go beyond this stereotyped image of American femininity' (189). Warren believes that Hawthorne's negative comments about certain of his women characters must be understood in the context of his condemnation of that particular behaviour whether it existed in men or in women: '... Hawthorne also criticizes pride in his male characters, and he censures anyone who devotes himself to an idea at the expense of human ties' (198–9). Thus Hawthorne's work lies 'outside the mainstream of American culture' (225) because Hawthorne did not believe in 'the characteristics of the American myth—individualism, emphasis on the self at the expense of the other, optimistic pursuit of individual achievement, and expansive faith in American progress' (225).

Warren details the importance of the impact of women on Hawthorne's work, particularly the influence of his wife Sophia, 'an independent and unusually accomplished woman' (204) without whose support he probably would not have become a successful writer. Because Hawthorne was always sympathetic to the women in his life, and not alienated from them, he was able, in Warren's view, 'to create female characters who stand out in American literature as women of substance and individuality' (230).

Jane P. Tompkins, in a chapter devoted to Hawthorne ('Masterpiece theater: the politics of Hawthorne's literary reputation'), in an extremely controversial work, *Sensational Designs*, has taken up the issue of why Hawthorne's work has become so popular. Tompkins wonders why his work, 'no more nor less highly regarded than the mass of popular magazine fiction of the time', has become canonized by 'teachers, scholars, and publishers'. She states that, although the evaluation of his work was supposedly unbiased, the cultural Brahmins of his time, who endorsed his work as 'genius' were men of the literary establishment whom Hawthorne knew personally.[7]

The readings of Hawthorne's novels which follow are based upon the critical tradition outlined here. Each chapter provides a brief historical or biographical orientation to the work discussed; my own reading of the work; and a synopsis of critical insights which helped me to develop a feminist reading. For feminists, and for this reader as well, the most important and controversial issue, and the issue which will preoccupy us in these pages, is whether or not Hawthorne himself was woman-loving, woman-hating, or ambivalent towards women, and whether or not the works themselves encode the misogyny that was prevalent in Hawthorne's own time.

CHAPTER THREE

Fanshawe, A Tale (1828)

In October of 1828, just about three years after his graduation from Bowdoin College in September of 1825, Nathaniel Hawthorne published a tale called *Fanshawe* with the Boston publishing house of Marsh and Capen.[1] According to his sister Elizabeth Hawthorne, her brother had decided to become a writer while he was still at college.[2] He had announced his decision in an 1821 letter to his mother: 'What do you think of my becoming an author, and relying for support upon my pen? How proud you would feel to see my works praised by the reviewers. . . .'[3] In all likelihood, the novel was written while he was still an undergraduate, or within a year after he graduated.[4]

The novel draws extensively upon Hawthorne's experiences as an undergraduate at Bowdoin, and it is one of the first, if not the first, novels about college life published in America.[5] It traces the fortunes of Fanshawe, a bookish, melancholy student, Edward Walcott, his more outward-going friend, who aspires to a literary career, and a young, naive and innocent woman, Ellen Langton, with whom they both fall in love. Ellen has been placed in the care of Dr Melmoth, the head of the college, by her father, the Merchant Langton, and she unknowingly becomes the target of his enemy, an evil man called Butler, who seeks revenge because Ellen's father, after caring for him, has abused him. The novel describes Butler's abduction of Ellen and his attempt to trick her into a marriage that will provide him with access to her father's fortunes, and the other characters' successful, but mock-heroic attempts to foil Butler's scheme. At the conclusion of the novel, Fanshawe renounces the world and drives himself into an early grave by his obsession with scholarship; Edward and Ellen marry and lead an obscure and ordinary life together.

Hawthorne paid for the publication of this work himself, a standard practice for fledgling authors at the time. The fee for publication, given Hawthorne's perennially precarious financial situation, was considerable, probably well in excess of the $100 that his sister Elizabeth remembers him paying. The novel was published anonymously, Hawthorne never publicly acknowledging in his lifetime that he was *Fanshawe*'s author; in later years, when his publisher James T. Fields asked him about the novel, Hawthorne 'spoke of it with great disgust'.[6] He suppressed the fact of his authorship so successfully that his wife, Sophia, after her husband's death, at first denied that the work was his, and later, after admitting that he might have deliberately withheld the fact of its existence, even from her, argued against reissuing the work, stating that if 'it does not equal his later works, and can do him no honor, I could wish that there were no traces of it on the earth'. The novel was not republished either in his lifetime, or during hers. It was reprinted in 1876, four years after his wife's death.

In *Fanshawe*, Ellen Langton is placed in the home of Dr Melmoth, a surrogate father, but this exposes her to great risk and she finds herself in the predicament of many young women in fairy tales: her coming into the Melmoth home seriously jeopardizes the status of Mrs Melmoth who soon unconsciously begins to act the role of the archetypal fairy-tale stepmother:[7] in fact, Dr Melmoth realizes that his wife is capable of vengeance towards Ellen.

At first, Mrs Melmoth welcomes the young woman as a potential source of unpaid labour: 'she might even be a help to me' (340) and Ellen, in fact, becomes Cinderella-like in the amount of work required of her: 'The nicer departments of cookery . . . were now committed to her care; and the Doctor's table was now covered with delicacies . . . '

(342). On the surface Mrs Melmoth does not wage war against this new object of her husband's affections, and even tries to like her. But Mrs Melmoth soon realizes that the young, beautiful, innocent, sweet Ellen poses a very serious threat to her, because Ellen soon assumes a position of supreme importance in her husband's affections:

> From the time that Ellen entered Doctor Melmoth's habitation, the sunny days seemed brighter and the cloudy ones less gloomy, than he had ever before known them. . . . She . . . became the blessing of his life—the rich recreation that he promised himself for hours of literary toil.
>
> . . . With Mrs. Melmoth, Ellen was not, of course, so great a favorite. (341)

And so Mrs Melmoth, unconsciously, begins to undermine the young woman's well-being. She does not attack her overtly nor does she treat her viciously; rather, she withholds from her the female protection and wisdom that are so necessary for a young woman in Ellen's position. At one point, Ellen does not know how to respond to a letter that Butler states is from her father, and in a chilling moment of insight she realizes that she has never been taught how to take care of herself, that there is absolutely no one in her life whom she can trust, and that, as a young, unmothered woman, she is terrifyingly alone:

> Mrs. Melmoth was the only female—excepting, indeed, the maid-servant—to whom it was possible to make the communication; and though Ellen at first thought of such a step, her timidity and her knowledge of the lady's character, did not permit her to venture upon it. (429)

She then thinks about the possibility of a male confidant, and realizes that she can trust no man. The narrator observes, quite correctly, that 'poor Ellen was consequently left without an adviser' (429).

In the novel, Ellen finds herself in what is a most precarious position for a young woman: her mother has died, and she is 'left alone with a widowed father' who would rather make his fortune than make a home for his motherless daughter: the Merchant Langton had '"set his heart to gather gold," and to this absorbing passion he sacrificed his domestic happiness' (338). Already, in this first novel, one can see Hawthorne exploring the ethical ramifications of leading a life of self-interest, an issue that he would explore again and again in the works of his maturity. Ellen had been given over to the care of relatives at such an early age, that 'she has never known her father' (403). Yet Langton, while committing the care of his daughter to a friend whom he had not seen for many years, *has* found the time and energy to act as surrogate parent to the youth Butler. The unspoken message about the worthlessness of female children is quite clear: Langton chooses to parent a male who is no relation to him; he abandons his daughter to the care of virtual strangers; his daughter has absolutely no economic value to him, and so he does not take personal responsibility for her well-being. She is a nuisance, a worthless piece of goods.

In fact, Langton is so unconcerned about her welfare, that when he arrives on the scene as Dr Melmoth and the others are pursuing Ellen, and he is informed about her abduction, all he can manage in the way of a response is 'a momentary convulsion' (419). Even though his daughter is in imminent peril, he does not rush to her assistance, nor does he spur the others on; instead, he tells Melmoth '*at your leisure*, I shall desire to hear the particulars of this unfortunate affair' (419; emphasis added)—which is certainly not the behaviour of a caring parent, but rather that of a self-involved man putting his own creature comforts ahead of her needs, even in an emergency. In fact, Ellen herself knows that she can expect nothing from him: she 'shrank with something like dread from the idea of meeting her father—stately, cold, and stern, as she could but imagine him' (428).

Nor can she expect very much from other male protectors. Once the Merchant Langton appears on the scene, Walcott perceives Ellen's rescue as a male/male battle for superiority; he was 'not well pleased at the sudden appearance of Ellen's father, and was little inclined to cooperate in any measures that he might adopt for her recovery . . . [;] he chose to be an independent ally, rather than a subordinate assistant' (421). Rather than joining forces with her father, Walcott deliberately conceals information about Ellen's whereabouts, and this move seriously jeopardizes their ability to rescue her. For Walcott, Ellen is an object to 'win' rather than a person who requires assistance. And when he realizes he is hungry, he does not continue his pursuit of her, as a romantic hero might; rather, he stops to eat an enormous meal, which he enjoys: 'nor were Edward's griefs and perplexities so absorbing, as to overcome the appetite of youth and health' (421). Ellen Langton has found herself a suitor with about as little concern for her needs as her father.

But Ellen is not the only woman in the novel who has been abandoned by a man. The Widow Butler has lived out a life of desperate poverty because her son, Ellen's abductor, left her some fifteen years before. During a walk, Ellen and Fanshawe decide to stop at a cottage for some refreshment. They see a 'half-starved cow . . . over the mouldering log fence' (348); it is a scene of immense deprivation:

> The occupants of the small and squalid apartment were two women, both of them elderly. . . . One . . . had the sallow look of long and wasting illness. . . . The other woman was bending over a small fire of decayed branches, . . . scarcely producing heat sufficient for the preparation of a scanty portion of food. (348)

The Widow Butler soon dies, 'raving mad' (409). When her son sees her dead body he feels a moment's 'deep repentance, for the misery he had brought upon his parent', for 'his neglect and cruelty [which] had poisoned his mother's life, and hastened her death' (435). Hawthorne seems to recognize, in this novel, that a widow's well-being is determined by her ability to control her own property. Hugh Crombie's wife, previously a widow, is not portrayed in the desperate condition of the Widow Butler: as the owner of an inn, she can take better care of herself.

A significant metaphor which deepens the meaning of the novel depicts Ellen as an object of prey. Because she stands to inherit her father's wealth, Ellen is potential prey in a society which passes a woman's money through to her husband. The innkeeper Hugh Crombie has married a propertied widow, and although he is not overly fond of his wife, 'the ceremony . . . made Hugh a landholder, a householder, and a substantial man' (371). Crombie and Butler discuss marrying a rich woman as 'a most excellent method of becoming a man of substance' (376) and Butler describes his plans to marry Ellen by compromising her virtue. To Butler, Ellen becomes the equivalent of the big fish that he is casting for when he first meets her by the stream. As she gazes at the fish in Butler's presence, there is a moment of intense eroticism between them as he entices her with 'his bold eye' to take 'his rod' (356) to catch the fish.

Ellen is, in fact, assaulted on all sides by virtually every character in the novel. As Fanshawe looks for her, 'his air . . . rather resembled the hunter, on the watch for his game . . . ' (362). And Walcott, because he considers her his personal property, when he becomes jealous becomes potentially dangerous (a trait which no critic has commented upon), and the target of his rage is Ellen: 'Her eye was sedulously averted from his; . . . it produced an effect upon his rather hasty temper, that might have manifested itself violently, but for the presence of Mrs. Melmoth . . .' (383). After he suspects that 'his pure and lovely Ellen—had degraded herself' with Butler, he becomes 'a perfect madman' (395), ' a raving maniac' (396), and it is only chance that again prevents Ellen from becoming the object of his rage. He

> manifested an impulse to break and destroy whatever chanced to be within his reach. . . . Then, seizing a tall heavy chair in each hand, he hurled them, with prodigious force, one through the window, and the other against a large looking-glass. (395)

There is an important recognition in *Fanshawe* that Ellen becomes the potential prey and victim of other abusive men because of the way her father has mistreated her. Because she has lived her life with an absent idealized father, her lack of real knowledge about male behaviour renders her incapable of discerning whether a man will be good to her or will abuse her. Like many abused, unparented, or abandoned children, Ellen feels powerless, and when she is abducted, she loses herself in a dreamworld of 'gorgeous vapors', 'a fairy land', and she longs 'for wings to visit it' (359)—feelings with which Hawthorne, given his own childhood, was no doubt familiar. Ellen has no real knowledge of how to take care of herself. Although her first impulse is to protect herself, to 'cry out for assistance', she tries, instead, to 'persuade herself that she was safe' (360), which is both a denial of her danger and an infantile attempt to control it, which puts her well-being at grave risk.

Hawthorne's tale is therefore far different from the stock plot of the sentimental or romantic novel:[8] in *Fanshawe*, Hawthorne describes, with great accuracy, the tendency of women who have been abandoned or abused by their fathers to repeat that experience with other men, and this is consistent with recent studies by feminist therapists.[9] Hawthorne understands that a woman like Ellen is not interested in male gentleness or protection, but rather in a man withholding affection from her and/or menacing her, which is why Butler is successful in abducting her, and why she marries Walcott. At one extremely significant moment, Butler piques her interest precisely because he withdraws from her—a repetition of her father's behaviour:

> With these words, . . . he drew back, and his form faded from her eyes. This precipitate retreat . . . was the most probable method, that he could have adopted, of gaining his end. He had awakened the strongest interest in Ellen's mind. (360)

Virtually all of the female/male relationships in *Fanshawe* are variations on the theme of male withdrawal.[10] Fanshawe cannot accept an intimate relationship with a woman, and instead he dies an early, self-inflicted death. Dr Melmoth is in constant retreat from his far more competent wife, and their relationship is like that of the Dame and her husband in Washington Irving's 'Rip Van Winkle'. Dr Melmoth has 'borne the matrimonial yoke' for nearly twenty years; his wife's 'domestic government often compelled him to call to mind such portions of the wisdom of antiquity, as relate to the proper endurance of the shrewishness of woman'. Rip retreats to nature; Dr Melmoth, to the quiet of his study, 'the only portion of the house, to which, since one fiercely repelled invasion, Mrs. Melmoth's omnipotence did not extend' (337).

In *Fanshawe*, there are two kinds of men: cold and/or vicious men who overtly tyrannize women, like Butler, Walcott, and the Merchant Langton; and men like Hugh Crombie (who assists Butler in abducting Ellen and then sabotages attempts to rescue her), Fanshawe, and Dr Melmoth, beneath whose sweet, jovial, or pathetic exteriors there exists a woman-hater. In the novel, women are either portrayed as naive and innocent, like Ellen, or they are monsters,[11] like Mrs Melmoth or the college bed-maker, 'a model of perfect ugliness . . . tall, raw-boned, huge-jointed, [a] double-fisted giantess, admirably fitted to sustain the part of Glumdalca, in the tragedy of Tom Thumb' (408). When they are passive, immobilized and helpless, they are idealized, as Ellen is in one scene, where she is perceived as 'blanched . . . as white as a lily, or as a marble statue, which for a moment she resembled, as she stood motionless in the center of the room' (392). But when they are active, they become monsters, objects to be ridiculed and punished. When Walcott is jealous of Ellen because she has undertaken a journey that he perceives as a rejection of him, he punitively remarks: 'Fifty years ago . . . my sweet Ellen would have been deemed a witch, for this trackless journey. Truly, I could wish I were a wizard, that I might bestride a broomstick, and follow her' (422). These telling images exhibit a competition, on Walcott's part, with Ellen for the power he perceives she possesses. And the language indicates that he wants to persecute her for her power, as witches were persecuted. But what he does not realize is that he is angry with her because he cares about her, and rather than accept the fact of his love, he rages against her and would like to destroy her. In this, he is the predecessor of Aylmer in 'The Birthmark'.

Fanshawe, like many other works of American literature written by men, encodes both a 'fear and envy of women'.[12] Throughout the novel there is a grudging acceptance, in certain male characters, of woman's power. But the source of woman's power is her innocence and what is believed to be her innate goodness, not her accomplishments. At the conclusion of the novel, Ellen's gentle nature changes Walcott, a potential wife-beater, into a nice man: 'Ellen's gentle, almost imperceptible, but powerful influence, drew her husband away from passions and pursuits that would have interfered with domestic felicity; and he never regretted the worldly distinction of which she thus deprived him' (460). Ellen's influence on Walcott is as great as the impact she has had on Dr Melmoth, but this assumption that a woman's nature is powerful enough to change a man's violence into good temper is problematic, for it makes a woman responsible for male behaviour and the quality of a man's life; and it absolves the men in the novel of any responsibility for their own behaviour, thereby blaming women (like Mrs Melmoth) if the men in their lives are not happy. At one point, for example, Ellen's mere presence is largely responsible for 'a general and very evident decline in the scholarship of the college' (342). The young men, instead of pursuing their 'severer studies', pen verses in Latin and Greek, which 'were strewn in the path where Ellen Langton was accustomed to walk' (342).

In *Dimity Convictions*, the historian Barbara Welter has described a 'popular cautionary tale in the nineteenth century' concerning the 'Merchant's Daughter who, faced with her father's ruin, was forced to make her own way in the world' (42). According to Welter, the tale encoded 'the ambivalence with which the New England conscience viewed the man of commerce: scorning his pursuit of money while regarding prosperity as a mark of Divine favor' (42). *Fanshawe* is a variation upon the theme, especially because one of the major elements of the tale is the role of the daughter as 'countervailing force to this dangerous materialism' (42). Because the Merchant Langton has abandoned his daughter, he has also abandoned the feminine principle through which he could have been saved from the consequences of his materialism.

In *Fanshawe*, the recognition that women have power is not always accompanied by a healthy respect for women; rather, it usually results in a desire for retribution (as in Walcott, Crombie and Butler) or for avoidance (as in Melmoth and Fanshawe).

In the novel, Hawthorne very often mocks the notion that men are inherently superior to women. Harley College, for example, only permits male students, but there is no indication that the men who attend the college benefit from the opportunity reserved for males of getting an education. Hawthorne seems to understand that education more often performs the élitist function of empowering a pre-selected stratum of society or gender than it serves the function of enlightening students. He seems to believe that human beings might be deluded in their belief that the process of education can change society for the better, for he states that the inhabitants of the farmhouses surrounding the college do 'not seem . . . to be in any degree influenced by the atmosphere of Harley College' (333). This is remarkable, for 'there is scarcely a family in the vicinity that has not provided, for at least one of its sons, the advantage of a "liberal education"' (334).

The chase scene in the novel is also a very serious challenge to assumptions of male superiority and gender-bound definitions of female and male roles and the scene is posed in the language of satire. When Melmoth discovers that Ellen is gone, all of the men in her life begin searching for her in a ludicrous serio-comic parody of such chases in gothic romances. Hugh Crombie lends Fanshawe an old horse that limps along; Melmoth is an inept knight errant who has lost the young woman placed in his care twice in two days; Walcott has armed himself with weapons that he does not know how to use.

Melmoth, in pursuing Ellen, realizes that his wife would

be far more likely to find her than he is, for he 'was altogether a child in the ways of the world, having spent his youth and early manhood in abstracted study' (415); Mrs Melmoth possesses the qualities to be an epic quester, and to rescue Ellen, not her husband or any of the other men who are chasing her. He wishes that he had invited 'Mrs. Melmoth to share in the adventure; this being an occasion where her firmness, decision, and confident sagacity—which made her a sort of domestic hedge-hog—would have been perfectly appropriate' (415-16).

Hawthorne suggests that the traditions of the sentimental romance, in which men rescue women, are ludicrous because they are based upon the fundamental misconception that all men by nature are capable beings and all women by nature need help. Hawthorne intimates that any man who behaves as if this assumption is in fact true will, in all likelihood, be sorely mistaken about his own potential for heroism. Walcott certainly perceives himself (incorrectly) as an epic quester, but Melmoth corrects him. Walcott compares himself to 'Tencer behind the shield of Ajax' but Melmoth interrupts the youth: 'No, no, young man', he says, 'I have left unfinished in my study a learned treatise . . . for whose sakes I must take heed to my safety' (417). Melmoth is not a hero, nor is Walcott, and for Melmoth his work, insignificant though it may be, is more important than any woman's life.

And so, in *Fanshawe*, no one really rescues Ellen. For a time, Ellen acts the part of the damsel in distress: 'she sat in the cave as motionless, for a time, as if she had herself been a part of the rock' (439) but after a time she wearies of the role, and simply walks out of the cave where Butler is keeping her: 'She determined . . . to attempt her own deliverance. . . . Gathering courage . . . she began to descend' (440-1). And in a scene which is an acerbic attack on the traditional conclusion of romantic and gothic novels, Fanshawe arrives on the scene, and rather than a struggle unto the death between a hero and a villain, Fanshawe tosses 'a small fragment of rock' (450) rather than a spear, and Butler, an inept villain if ever there was one, grasps 'at a twig' as he climbs the precipice to attack Fanshawe, and because it 'was too slenderly rooted to sustain his weight' (451), it gives way, and he falls to his death.

Fanshawe therefore satirizes the tradition of the sentimental novel and the romance, in which a young woman like Ellen, often motherless or parentless, is subjected to an assault on her virtue by a reprobate, and who must demonstrate, under the most difficult circumstances, the integrity of her principles and her fitness for marriage. In the strictest sense, Ellen has failed the test and has become a fallen woman; Walcott, her suitor, believes that she has been defiled by going off with Butler. But, in an inversion of the stock ending, he marries her anyway and they lead a 'long life of calm and quiet bliss' (460).

Judy Little in *Comedy and the Woman Writer* describes a tradition of women's comedy 'which implies . . . a . . . radical reordering of social structures, a real rather than temporary and merely playful redefinition of sex identity . . . '(2). Little's work suggests that novels written by outsiders do not share the society's norms because outsiders do not have access to power and are therefore critical of a structure which keeps them powerless. Hawthorne's *Fanshawe* is best understood as a comic novel written by an outsider which mocks social norms presumed to be sacred by those with access to power in a society. In this sense, *Fanshawe* is in the tradition of the woman's comic novel. Because he was a widow's son, Hawthorne experienced, at first hand, the powerlessness of a widow (and of women in general), her lack of access to economic well-being, her (and her children's) dependence on the whim of male relatives. And he might have experienced, as well, the abuse of patriarchal power in the household of Robert Manning. It is possible that Robert Manning abused Hawthorne at some point in his life; the two shared a bed when Hawthorne lived in the Manning household.

For many years, until he was able to earn money for himself, Hawthorne, like the women in his society, was utterly powerless, utterly dependent upon his uncle. Ellen's experiences in *Fanshawe*, as well as the experiences of all of the women in the novel, are a fictional transcription of Hawthorne's own experiences. Hawthorne, like Ellen Langton, did not know his father, who died in Surinam when Hawthorne was eight. Ellen's father is a merchant seaman; Hawthorne's father was a sailor, and it is highly likely that Hawthorne perceived his death as an abandonment. When Hawthorne was writing the novel, Robert Manning, his uncle, upon whom his family was economically dependent, made it impossible for him to see his widowed mother for seven years. Hawthorne's guilt and sense of responsibility for his mother's well-being are in all likelihood fictionally rendered in these scenes depicting the Widow Butler's mistreatment by her son, but Hawthorne, unlike Butler, was powerless to help his mother.[13]

The reason that Hawthorne understands so well the psychic processes of women like Ellen is that he experienced those feelings himself. One can hypothesize that he projected his own experiences into the characters of women in his novels, because those feelings of dependence and powerlessness were the norm for women in his society, and were considered abnormal in men.

The only way for Hawthorne to explore those feelings was under the cover of his female characters. But he encodes, as well, in the characters of the men in *Fanshawe*, his rage at women, his blaming women for his own powerlessness, a phenomenon described by Dorothy Dinnerstein in *The Mermaid and the Minotaur* wherein the child's first experience with betrayal is at the hands of a woman. But Hawthorne, in a rare admission for a male author, understands, as well, that social forces and not his mother are to blame for his dependence. Even so, the character of Fanshawe, who is suicidally depressed, must be taken as a fictional projection of the self-destructive tendencies of a man like Hawthorne, who, enraged at his lack of power, like so many women, turns that rage into depression, an assault on the self.

Fanshawe was generally well-received upon its publication.[14] Sarah Josepha Hale, editor of *Ladies' Magazine*, recommended that her readers buy the novel (42). Both the anonymous reviewer for the *Yankee and Boston Literary Gazette* and William Leggett, of *The Critic*, believed that the novel presaged a future greatness for its author; Leggett wrote: 'The mind that produced this little, interesting volume, is capable of making great and rich additions to our native literature . . . '(43,45). Some reviews, like the one in the *Boston Weekly Messenger*, commented adversely upon the derivative nature of the novel, and stated that the 'characters in *Fanshawe*', with the exception of Hugh Crombie, the innkeeper 'are not wholly original' (44). But perhaps the most negative critical notice appeared in the *New England Galaxy* for 31 October 1828; it read: '*Fanshawe*. . . . A love story . . . like ten thousand others, [with] a mystery, an elopement; a villain, a father, a tavern, almost a duel, a horrible death, and—heaven save the mark! . . . an end' (41).

Many twentieth-century critics have been far less generous in their assessment of Hawthorne's first novel than his contemporaries. Some, like Hyatt Howe Waggoner, believe that the novel is 'totally unsuccessful and immature' (25), largely because the work was 'his experiment with the fictional formulas popular in the 1820's', 'the melodrama of the sentimental Gothic tale' (252). Randall Stewart, one of Hawthorne's biographers, has called it 'a novel of indifferent merit' (27). Others, like Carl Bode, Eric Homberger, and Terence Martin, although they do not necessarily believe that the work is successful, read the novel as an early and less sophisticated exploration of a theme that would preoccupy Hawthorne in his mature works—the negative consequences of self-imposed isolation—and they see his character Fanshawe (who denies the possibility of being reborn through Ellen's love) as a precursor of later Hawthorne heroes, for example Dimmesdale in *The Scarlet Letter*. Millicent Bell states that *Fanshawe* is Hawthorne's earliest expression of a central theme, that 'art (or the scholar's arduous devotion) is an isolating occupation, which destroys the capacity for normal happiness' (181).

Critics like Robert Sattelmeyer, Jesse Sidney Goldstein,

and Neal Frank Doubleday have investigated the sources of *Fanshawe* in Hawthorne's college reading.[15] Sattelmeyer sees the novel as profoundly influenced by writings of the Scottish common-sense school of philosophy, such as Adam Smith's *Theory of Moral Sentiments*, and he states that the novel emphasizes 'the innate impulses of men to do good' (201–2). Goldstein describes the similarities between *Fanshawe* and Charles Robert Maturin's *Melmoth the Wanderer* from which Hawthorne derived the name Dr Melmoth: both novels are about young women who have been abandoned; in both novels, the hero dies either through an overt suicide or through suicidal behaviour (1–8). Doubleday has commented upon the profound impact of Sir Walter Scott upon the tale and has stated that Hawthorne's aim in this first effort was to write an Americanized version of the Waverley novels.[16]

Nina Baym is the only feminist to date who has developed a reading of *Fanshawe*,[17] and although she views the work as an artistic failure, she explores the ways in which Hawthorne has 'Americanized' and softened the gothic tradition in his creation of the novel. Observing that gothic tales often describe 'female misery', her work alerts feminist readers to the ways in which that traditional form has been linked to the reality of female suffering in a male-dominated social structure. She examines the fact that Hawthorne has reinterpreted the traditional gothic heroine in the person of Ellen Langton, whose 'combination of practicality and fluff . . . heralds the "American girl"' character (108) that a number of other critics, such as Judith Fetterley and Leslie Fiedler, have found to be a constant feature of novels written by men in America.

In addition to Baym, there are a number of critics whose work is extremely useful in developing a feminist reading. Leslie Fiedler, James R. Mellow, and Frederick Crews all explore how Hawthorne's novel encodes a resistance towards mature heterosexual love and marriage. Crews sees this resistance as a projection of Hawthorne's own ambivalent feelings towards women; he reads Fanshawe as a 'Hawthorneian bystander' who 'has escaped a relationship for which he was temporarily unsuited' and he sees the romance as satisfying two deeply-felt, though conflicting fantasies of the author: 'one of heroism and amorous success [which he projects onto the persona of Walcott] and another of throbbing self-abnegation [which he projects onto the persona of Fanshawe]'. For Crews, the 'net effect is more or less what we gather from Hawthorne's early letters and journals: he continues to cherish his own dream of undying fame but senses that it would be dissipated by a happy marriage' (162).

Fiedler sees *Fanshawe* as a novelistic failure, but he states that within this experiment Hawthorne 'invents the protagonists that inform almost all the rest of his work', especially the character of Fanshawe, whom he describes as 'psychologically impotent' (227), unable to 'get the girl' (226). Like Baym, Fiedler believes that the novel evokes 'stereotypes right out of the stock of the genteel sentimental novel: the depraved Seducer, the virtuous Maiden, the brave young lover ... plus the supernumerary male rescuer. ...' But Fiedler believes that Hawthorne has weakened the traditional tale; he criticizes the sentimentality of the effort which is marked by Hawthorne's incapacity to let the form work itself through to its usual conclusion in a striking demonstration of what Mary Ellmann has referred to as phallic criticism; he interprets the ending as a 'latter-day failure of nerve before the prospect of letting any real young lady get raped' (225).

Both E. Cifelli and James G. Janssen have explored the comic elements of Hawthorne's tale. Janssen has stated that there are deliberately comic dimensions to Hawthorne's rhetoric, that the 'circumlocution, rhetorical excess, and ironic understatement ... have the effect of puffing up a subject matter and pointing out incongruities ... '(24). Since much of the tale has to do with assumptions of male dominance and male privilege within an educational system and a mercantile economy, and also with male behaviour in response to female distress, the feminist reader can apply Janssen's analysis to determine whether Hawthorne's prose style mocks gender-bound determinations of access to education, power, and privilege. Janssen also observes that there is 'an attempt', on Hawthorne's part, 'through humorously inflated language to see things in their true perspective, diminishing the pretentious and elevating the lowly . . . '(25). Feminist readers can alert themselves both to the ways in which Hawthorne has exposed the pretentiousness of his characters—the students, the innkeeper, the merchant, the head of the college—and the ways in which he has dignified the suffering of his lowly characters—the widow, the wife, the abandoned daughter, the abandoned mother.

Cifelli observes that Hawthorne mocks Dr Melmoth's attempt to become a 'knight-errant' to help Ellen when she is in trouble and he cautions readers not to take the work as a straightforward romantic or gothic novel. He reads Melmoth as 'perfectly ludicrous, a modern but comically reluctant Don Quixote' (16). The feminist reader of *Fanshawe* can extend Cifelli's insight by regarding the *entire* novel as a serio-comic parody of the romantic and gothic traditions that were enormously popular in Hawthorne's day.

Fanshawe is a fascinating document for the feminist student of Hawthorne. It provides an extremely accurate portrait of the realities of the lives of women in America during and prior to the time that Hawthorne was writing the tale, and it describes yet criticizes the prevailing myths about the nature of women which governed the roles assigned to women and how women and men related to one another during the nineteenth century. It is an ironic critique of and commentary upon how popular novelistic traditions misrepresented human experience: it both draws upon and criticizes the tradition of the domestic novel, usually written by women; and it spoofs the gothic tradition. And finally, *Fanshawe* can be read as a fictive account of Hawthorne's mother's life experience as a widow, and it can be read as an illuminating autobiographical transcription of Hawthorne's personal experience with the economic and psychic ramifications of being a widow's son during the nineteenth century. In this regard, *Fanshawe* is a novel especially appropriate for our times, when 'the feminization of poverty' is forcing an increasing number of the world's women and their children to live in desperate poverty or dependent upon the largesse of a male-dominated economic system in conditions that are becoming more and more equivalent to those in which Elizabeth Hawthorne and her children lived their lives during the nineteenth century, more and more like the lives of many of the women described in *Fanshawe*.

Fanshawe is more challenging to gender-determined cultural norms than anything written by other male writers at the time; it is a far more radical critique of presumptions about maleness and femaleness than anything Hawthorne would write in his maturity. It is, in fact, a woman-identified novel.

CHAPTER FOUR

The Scarlet Letter, a Romance (1850)

On Saturday, 27 July 1844, Nathaniel Hawthorne made an entry in his notebook that was the germ for his most famous and most critically acclaimed novel, *The Scarlet Letter*: 'The life of a woman, who by old colony law, was condemned always to wear the letter A, sewed on her garment, in token of her having committed adultery.'[1]

Between the publication of *Fanshawe* in 1828, until the time he began working on *The Scarlet Letter*, in 1849, when he was in his mid-forties, Hawthorne had confined his writing to short works,[2] many of which were published in periodicals such as *The Token* and the *Salem Gazette*, and later collected in *Twice-Told Tales* and *Mosses from an Old Manse*.[3] Although Hawthorne was prolific, he found it impossible to support his family on the paltry amounts he earned from his writing—he was paid only 'an average of $1.00 per page'[4] for his contributions to *The Token*—so that by the time he began *The Scarlet Letter*, he and Sophia had experienced periods of financial destitution, which had forced them to move in with Hawthorne's mother, then living on Mall Street in Salem, and had led Hawthorne to accept, on 3 April 1846, the position of Surveyor of the Custom-House in Salem.[5]

Hawthorne worked at the Custom-House until his dismissal, on 8 June 1849, as a result of the Whigs electoral victory. His wife, Sophia, 'greeted the first news of his dismissal with the remark, "Oh, then, you can write your book!"'

It was an extremely difficult time for him, for, on 30 July, his mother died. On the day before her death, in a journal entry, Hawthorne described the time that he spent at her bedside as 'the darkest hour I ever lived'. After her death he became seriously ill, but in September, after he recovered, he began writing *The Scarlet Letter* in 'response to his mother's death',[6] and as a kind of elegy to her. Like his heroine Hester Prynne, Elizabeth Hawthorne had become pregnant with her first child outside of marriage and had been socially ostracized; like Hester, his mother was husbandless, a single parent, raising her offspring alone, on the fringes of society. But it is also likely that his mother's death provided a kind of creative release, for he worked 'with an intensity that almost frightened his wife, and with a speed that brought the book to completion before the year ended'.[7] His wife Sophia certainly made the writing of the novel possible because without the money she had saved, 'a hundred and fifty dollars in bills, in silver, even in coppers',[8] her earnings from her decorative work, Hawthorne would have had to find another form of employment. The novel was composed quickly, and was completed on 3 February 1850.[9]

'The Custom-House' which serves as an introduction to and provides a frame for *The Scarlet Letter* was intended by Hawthorne to be a deliberate act of aggression and revenge against the Whigs who were responsible for his dismissal from his post. As author of the piece, he saw himself as a 'hunter', and he described the act of writing as the loading of a 'gun with a bullet and several buckshot'; reading his work, moreover, would 'kill the public . . . with my biggest and heaviest lump of lead'.[10] 'The Custom-House' is a savage, even vicious, satire against government service, and the kind of men who enter it. The Custom-House officers talk 'with that lack of energy that distinguishes the occupants of alms-houses, and all other human beings who depend for subsistence on charity . . . or any thing else but their own independent exertions' (7); the veterans under Hawthorne's orders, largely Whigs, whom he has not dismissed, although he should have, 'go lazily about what they termed duty, and, at their own leisure and convenience, betake themselves to bed again' (13). Hawthorne clearly feels that if he has tolerated them, and allowed them to continue in government service, because he 'could never quite find in my heart to act upon the knowledge' (14) that they should be dismissed, the Whigs should have allowed him to retain his position.

Hawthorne reserves his most acid attack for the Permanent Inspector, animal-like, with 'no soul, no heart, no mind; nothing, as I have already said, but instincts' (18), whose main attribute was his ability to recollect 'the ghosts of bygone meals', 'while all the subsequent experience of our race ... had gone over him with as little permanent effect as the passing breeze' (19).

Although Hawthorne makes it quite clear that he believes that he has been betrayed by *male* politicians, and that he intends to take his revenge upon them, none the less, the image which introduces 'The Custom-House' and dominates it, is the image of the American eagle, which Hawthorne depicts as a negative *female* image. It is worth quoting in its entirety, because the tale that Hawthorne tells of betrayal by the political system is enacted against the backdrop of this image of female betrayal. Over the entrance to the Custom-House,

> hovers an enormous specimen of the American eagle, with outspread wings, a shield before her breast, and, . . . a bunch of intermingled thunderbolts and barbed arrows in each claw. With the customary infirmity of temper that characterizes this unhappy fowl, she appears, by the fierceness of her beak and eye and the general truculency of her attitude, to threaten mischief to the inoffensive community; and especially to warn all citizens, careful of their safety, against intruding on the premises which she overlooks with her wings. Nevertheless, vixenly as she looks, many people are seeking, at this very moment, to shelter themselves under the wing of the federal eagle; imagining, I presume, that her bosom has all the softness and snugness of an eider-down pillow. But she has no great tenderness, even in her best of moods, and, sooner or later, . . . is apt to fling off her nestlings with a scratch of her claw, a dab of her beak, or a rankling wound from her barbed arrows. (5)

This image is extraordinary not only because it transforms the American eagle (the symbol of American might and strength) into a *female* image, but also because the effect of this transformation is subtly yet bitterly misogynist. It states that this female eagle is potentially and unpredictably vicious 'to the inoffensive community' precisely because she is female, and it is in the nature of females to be unpredictable; moreover, this female eagle is doubly vicious and unpredictable because she is an *unhappy* female who might lash out, with her 'thunderbolts' and her 'barbed arrows' at any one, at any time, whether or not they deserve it.

What Hawthorne accomplishes by rendering the national American symbol as female, is, in effect, a shifting of the responsibility and blame for his dismissal from the Custom-House away from the men who were responsible (and, by extension, away from the male-dominated patriarchal political system). Instead, despite his acerbic and rancorous remarks about men in government service, it is clear from this image of the female federal eagle, that, at some deep level, Hawthorne experienced his dismissal as *maternal* rejection, rather than as the result of a male political wrangle. Thus, the female federal eagle becomes the bad mother. She does not offer 'great tenderness, even in her best of moods', but rather flings her nestlings (one of whom was Hawthorne himself) from the nest 'with a scratch of her claw', or, even worse, 'a rankling wound from her barbed arrows' (5). This image subtly, but effectively, indicates that, at some deep level, Hawthorne irrationally blamed his mother for having abandoned him through her death, and that he also blamed her for losing his position at the Custom-House. What the feminist reader of 'The Custom-House' must note is how this image misrepresents political power as female, and how it blames a maternal figure for what is, in reality, the action of a male-dominated political machine.

Near the beginning of 'The Custom-House', Hawthorne announces that one of his reasons for writing the sketch is to 'put myself in my true position as editor' (4) of Hester Prynne's tale, and to explain 'how a large portion of the following pages came into my possession, and as offering proofs of authenticity of a narrative contained therein' (4). Hawthorne describes finding barrels in the second storey of the Custom House, containing bundles of documents of Jonathan Pue, a surveyor and local antiquarian, which could be used for 'a regular history of Salem' (31). In the bundle, Hawthorne discovers 'a certain affair of fine red cloth, much worn and faded . . . [which] on careful examination assumed the shape of a letter. It was the capital A' (31) together with 'a small roll of dingy paper' containing 'a reasonably complete explanation of the whole affair' (32).

This fictive posture of Hawthorne as editor of an historical document is an attempt to persuade the reader that the story that he tells, though embellished, is in effect an authentic, if not true account of Hester Prynne's fate in Puritan New England, and that the novel is the 'representation of a mode of life not heretofore described' (4): 'What I contend for is the authenticity of the outline' (33). Thus Hester's story comes to represent a model for describing the ways in which women who deviated from Puritan law were treated in Puritan New England and a model for understanding the character of the male élite Puritan oligarchy.

Although, ostensibly, *The Scarlet Letter* is a novel about a woman, what is insisted upon in the purported autobiography at the beginning of the novel, is that writing the history of a culture, that writing the history of a woman's fate within a culture, is, and ought to be, a strictly male enterprise. Attributing Hester's tale to the researches of Jonathan Pue effectively serves to write out his wife Sophia's, his mother Elizabeth's, and his daughter Una's relationship to the creation of the novel. If Hawthorne's prologue is, in fact, what it purports to be—an autobiographical account of how *The Scarlet Letter* came into being—it seems curious that Hawthorne would create Surveyor Pue and then credit him for the novel, rather than the women to whom he was indebted. Why bother to invent the fiction of the autobiographical frame at all if the autobiographical frame is, in fact, a fiction? In fact, what Hawthorne is doing, although he may not be aware of it, is creating his own autobiography by disavowing the facts of his life: he is creating what he would like the reader to know about himself: he is creating himself even as he creates Hester Prynne.

So convincing is Hawthorne's ploy that the reader rarely notices that the introduction provides a fascinating account of how the writing of romance or history *must* be articulated as if it proceeds from male to male even when (or perhaps especially when) women are the subject of that history, even when women have, in fact, made the writing of that work possible. In one very important scene, Hawthorne has a fantasy about Pue handing him Hester's story, and he describes Pue here as a ghostly father:

> With his own ghostly hand, the obscurely seen, but majestic figure had imparted to me the scarlet symbol, and the little roll of explanatory manuscript. With his own ghostly voice, he had exhorted me, on the sacred consideration of my filial duty and reverence towards him,—who might reasonably regard himself as my official ancestor to bring his mouldy and moth-eaten lucubrations before the public. (33)

Thus, Hawthorne does not perceive the function of telling his tale as serving the causes of women's history; rather, Hawthorne is using one woman's story to serve the purposes of *male* history, both his own and men in general—a fact that has been overlooked by feminist literary critics. As Pue's ghost instructs Hawthorne: '. . . I charge you, in this matter of old Mistress Prynne, give to your predecessor's memory the credit which will be rightfully its due!' (33–4).

The fundamental assumption about the nature of history that is embedded here is that woman's history is, and ought to be, the *property* of the male historian. Indeed, in the first moments of the novel, as Hester is about to emerge from the prison, Hawthorne uses the word 'narrative' to describe her: just as she is about to emerge from the jail, so is 'our narrative, . . . about to issue from that inauspicious portal' (48). She is not a character, she is a narrative, and in the language that Hawthorne insists upon, Hester and the narrative are, in fact, the same.

Moreover it is absolutely necessary that this history be presented as if it were authentic *especially if* that account grossly misrepresents woman's history, as the life story of Hester Prynne in *The Scarlet Letter* grossly distorts the fate of women who committed adultery in Puritan New England. In one very important sense, depicting Hester's strength and her resilience in the face of her punishment serves to nullify the effects of such persecution. If Hester could endure, and triumph (as women who were persecuted for adultery surely did not), then the negative consequences of the persecution itself are blunted, and the persecuting fathers rendered less virulent than they in fact were.

Critics, such as Charles Ryskamp and William Charvat have documented the fact that Hawthorne read widely in the history of Puritan New England of the 1640s, and that his notebooks indicate his concern with getting the details of that time precisely correct. Sources such as Caleb H. Snow's *History of Boston* and Joseph Felt's *Annals of Salem* were read and used 'to create an authentic picture of the seventeenth century'.[11] But despite Hawthorne's concern for accurate details, what has been glossed is the fundamental inaccuracy of the substance of Hawthorne's tale. Although Hawthorne would have known that Plymouth law decreed two whippings and the wearing of the letters 'AD' on the arm or back of the adulteress,[12] he has omitted the whippings from his romance and has Hester embellish the 'A' into an object of great beauty; although 'Governor John Winthrop's journal of 1644 records the execution, in the Bay Colony, of Mary Latham, eighteen, who having married an "ancient man . . . whom she had no affection unto," committed adultery with "divers young men"'[13] as the fate of the adulteress, Hawthorne writes, instead, how Hester's punishment is to endure the stares of the townspeople as she stands on the scaffold; although a real Hester Craford, in '1668 was found guilty of fornication', a 'lesser sin than adultery', and was 'whipped, and had her child taken from her', Hester is neither whipped, nor deprived of her child (xxvii); although Felt's *Annals* records that in 1694, 'adultery was punishable by an hour on the gallows, forty stripes' (xxvii), and the wearing of a capital 'A', Hawthorne has omitted the forty stripes from his tale. At the end of the novel, Hawthorne has Hester returning to the place of her punishment and *voluntarily* resuming her persecution, for 'not the sternest magistrate of that iron period would have imposed it,—[she] resumed the symbol of which we have related so dark a tale' (262). This is certainly a bizarre touch—to state that even the most iron-handed Puritan magistrate would not persecute her is falsifying history; to state that she willingly puts on the letter 'A' makes her *self*- persecuting, rather than persecuted. If Hawthorne, as he himself stated, was striving for *authenticity* in writing Hester's tale, *The Scarlet Letter* must be adjudged a woefully inaccurate failure.

In fact, even rendering the character of Dimmesdale as so pathetic, so ineffectual, so self-destructive effectively serves to dim the ferocity of his historical counterparts: it is impossible to read Hawthorne's Dimmesdale and conceptualize the Puritan oligarchy as avenging avatars. Instead of a persecuting angel, inspired by the wrath of the righteous, we are given the portrait of a bumbling lover, a portrait of a man who beats himself with 'a bloody scourge' (144), who punishes *himself* for hiding his sin, rather than a man who persecutes others.

Hawthorne substitutes Dimmesdale's refusal to acknowledge the fact of his paternity (which is surely interesting in light of Hawthorne's biography) and Chillingworth's probing into the secrets of Dimmesdale's heart as greater evils than the evils suffered by those persecuted by Puritan justice! And so, in the context of *The Scarlet Letter*, in a fascinating reversal of the facts of history, Dimmesdale, the representative of the Puritan state and Puritan power in the novel, becomes more sinned against than sinning—he is described as the 'victim . . . for ever on the rack' (140)—and his victimization at the hands of Chillingworth becomes of greater consequence and has more dire results than Hester's punishment! Hawthorne, in his revisionist history, thus substitutes a portrait of a male victim for an accurate portrait of a female victim of the Puritan oligarchy.

One of his primary arguments that blunts the effect of the persecution of women is that grief and suffering, rather than being destructive to a woman, is, in fact, ennobling, so long as she does not become a social reformer as a result of it: Hester wears 'a halo of misfortune' (53); when Hester sees Pearl's gaiety, what she wants for her, is 'a grief that should deeply touch her, and thus humanize and make her capable of sympathy' (185).

As the novel progresses, Hawthorne subtly shifts the blame for what happens to Chillingworth and to Dimmesdale onto the shoulders of Hester. The effect of this is to render Hester completely responsible for the physical, emotional and spiritual well-being of the men in her life. Chillingworth tells her 'Woman, woman, thou art accountable for this' (194) and Dimmesdale repeatedly insists that his salvation is her responsibility: 'Think for me Hester! Thou art strong' (196). In one very important scene, Chillingworth blames Hester, and not the rigid system of Puritan justice, or his own actions, for Dimmesdale's slow demise: he tells her 'you [Hester] cause him to die daily a living death' (171); and she accepts the blame for Chillingworth's obsession with revenge—when he asks her who is responsible, she says 'It was myself' (173) just as she accounts herself responsible for Dimmesdale: she becomes 'sensible of the deep injury for which she was responsible to this unhappy man, in permitting him to lie for so many years' (192). Thus, Hester, the person with the least amount of real power in the novel is made, symbolically, the person with the most power, and the most responsibility for the outcome of the tale. This move deflects attention away from the reality of Hester's utter powerlessness in the Puritan scheme. Just as Hawthorne fixes our attention on Dimmesdale's dying, and on Hester's heroism and her responsibility for the well-being of the men in her life, to blunt the facts of Puritan history, so he employs a similar strategy when, in 'The Custom-House', his symbolic language presents *his* persecution at the hands of the Whigs as having a greater consequence than Hester's suffering: he aligns himself with the benighted Dimmesdale when he

describes writing Hester's story 'from beyond the grave' (44), and he states, in bold, attention-getting letters, that her tale 'may be considered as the POSTHUMOUS PAPERS OF A DECAPITATED SURVIVOR' (43); the 'A' that he finds in the pack of old papers sears *his* breast, not hers.

In 'The Custom-House', Hawthorne describes his very real connection with the historical figures in the novel by relating his family history, 'the deep and aged roots which my family has struck into the soil' (8). It is important to note that he conceptualizes his family history in completely male terms; in the family tree that he outlines here for himself, not one woman is mentioned. He describes the 'figure of that first ancestor, invested by family tradition with a dim and dusky grandeur, was present to my boyish imagination, as far back as I can remember' (9) and how the figure of this 'grave, bearded, sable-cloaked, and steeple-crowned progenitor,—who came so early with his Bible and his sword' haunted his imagination. Hawthorne describes this forebear as a 'bitter persecutor', and he relates how his son 'inherited the persecuting spirit' by making 'himself so conspicuous in the martyrdom of the witches' (9).

Although Hawthorne admits that his male ancestors were 'bitter persecutors', and although he admits that they indulged in 'cruelties', he blunts the effect of this admission by various narrative strategies. One strategy is to describe actual historical events as hypothetical events. For example, he does not describe the persecution of heterodox believers and so-called witches as *having* taken place: he describes those persecutions as if they *might* have taken place: 'It might be, that an Antinomian, a Quaker, or other heterodox religionist, was to be scourged out of town . . . It might be, too, that a witch like old Mistress Hibbins . . . was to die upon the gallows' (48). Or he blunts the effect of persecution, when he describes it, by employing neutral language: offenders are not beaten, they are 'corrected at the whipping-post' (49); the pillory is 'an agent in the promotion of good citizenship' (55); Hester's 'A' is not a punishment, but a 'fitting decoration to the apparel which she wore' (53).

Thus, the effect of Hawthorne's description of the Puritan oligarchs is to render them as having been simply intolerant men, rather than as sadists and misogynists, the only conclusion that can be reached after reading a history of the Hawthorne family, such as that by Vernon Loggins. In Loggins, the bearded, sable-cloaked Hathorne's typical punishments are described: he 'ordered a constable to cut off a convicted burglar's ear and brand the letter B on his forehead'; he sentenced a woman accused of fornication to a whipping, but simply fined a man who routinely beat his wife; he ordered into slavery the children of Quakers; he ordered 'hangings, the cutting off of men's ears, the boring of holes through women's tongues with red hot irons' and the starving to death of imprisoned Quakers (63). Nor can Hathorne's punishments be explained away by stating that they were typical of the time: indeed, so excessive was his zeal, that in 1661, because of his behaviour, Charles II commanded that any case involving a Quaker should be transferred to English courts. Hathorne's son was equally guilty of excesses; by 1692, as the magistrate responsible for the preliminary hearings in the Salem witchcraft trials, he had crowded the prisons with 'supposed witches and wizards'; on 19 July 1692 five women were hanged.[14]

Hawthorne's purpose in writing *The Scarlet Letter* is overtly announced in 'The Custom-House'. He states:

> I know not whether these ancestors of mine bethought themselves to repent, and ask pardon of Heaven for their cruelties; or whether they are not groaning under the heavy consequences of them, in another state of being. At all events, I, the present writer, as their representative, hereby take shame upon myself for their sakes, and pray that any curse incurred by them ... may now and henceforth be removed. (9–10).

The act of writing the novel, will, therefore, exculpate Hawthorne's Puritan forebears 'now and henceforth'. It is no wonder, therefore, given his self-admitted reason for writing the novel, why he revises what Hester's fate would have been into the tale that he tells. In order to remove the burden of guilt and responsibility from his male forebears, he must rewrite woman's history. Instead of presenting a vicious tale of brandings and beatings, what Hawthorne presents instead is the pargeted[15] tale of Hester Prynne: 'her beauty shone out, and made a halo of the misfortune and ignominy in which she was enveloped' (53).

Hawthorne's principal strategy, at the beginning of the novel itself, is to deflect attention away from the Puritan patriarchs who have voted Hester's punishment, the patriarchs who have made the laws and who enforce them. They scarcely exist as far as the novel is concerned. Rather, as Hester Prynne emerges from the jail, Hawthorne focuses all of his narrative attention, and for several pages, upon the vengeful response of the Puritan *women*. They take 'a peculiar interest in whatever penal infliction might be expected to ensue' (50). In the novel, it is not the oligarchs, Hawthorne's forebears, who punish, it is the goodwives who demand justice:

> 'Goodwives', said a hard-featured dame of fifty, 'I'll tell ye a piece of my mind. It would be greatly for the public behoof, if we women, being of mature age and church-members in good repute, should have the handling of such malefactresses as this Hester Prynne. What think ye, gossips? If the hussy stood up for judgment before us five, that are now here in a knot to gather, would she come off with such a sentence as the worshipful magistrates have awarded? Marry, I trow not!' (51)

Although Hawthorne appears to be arguing for gender-determined punishment, he is also stating that the male judges who did exist were fairer than any woman would have been. A man in the crowd who overhears the women says 'is there no virtue in woman, save what springs from a wholesome fear of the gallows?' (52). And Hawthorne states that the uglier a woman is, the more vengeance she would exact from criminals: 'the ugliest as well as the most pitiless of these self-constituted judges' says 'This woman has brought shame upon us all and ought to die. Is there not law for it?' (51). All the vengeance at the beginning of the novel has been female; when a beadle finally appears, he seems far less severe than the women; in contrast to their graphic desire to 'put the brand of a hot iron on Hester Prynne's forehead' (51), he simply 'prefigured and represented in his aspect the whole dismal severity of the Puritanic code of law' (52).

This is a fascinating strategy. Hawthorne denies history by misrepresenting Hester's punishment as if it would have been essentially fair and judicious. Then he argues that if women had had political power, they would have been harsher to adulteresses than his fictional Puritan leaders had been to Hester. Hawthorne therefore creates a romance about judicious Puritan rule which denies the reality of the abuse of power by Puritan rulers, and then he uses the fiction he has created to argue that men are essentially more fair-minded than women would be! This literary strategy, though highly persuasive, is extraordinarily illogical and misleading for Hawthorne draws ethical conclusions about justice being fair-minded if it is male, and vengeful if it is female from a universe which he himself has created, and which is a misrepresentation of historical reality.

In the context of the Puritan cosmology developed in *The Scarlet Letter*, Hester Prynne is enormously concerned about what will happen to her child Pearl, as well she should be because the children of miscreants were not treated well in Puritan New England. Throughout the novel, Pearl is repeatedly associated with the devil, with evil, with sin, and with witchcraft: her looks are 'perverse' and 'malicious' (92); she is an 'imp of evil' (93), 'fiend-like', an 'evil spirit' (97), 'a shadowy reflection of evil' (94), a 'demon offspring' (99), a 'demon-child' (100); there is a 'fire in her' (101); her cries are 'a witch's anathemas in some unknown tongue' (94), she is a 'little baggage [who] hath witchcraft in her' (116), there is 'witchcraft in little Pearl's eyes' (154); she is 'a shadowy reflection of evil' (94), the 'effluence of her mother's lawless passion' (165); her imaginary playmates are 'the puppets of Pearl's witchcraft' (95). And Hawthorne makes it clear that she has inherited these tendencies from her mother: although, *in utero*, Pearl's character was at first unblemished, her 'mother's impassioned state had been the medium through which were transmitted to the unborn infant the rays of its mortal life; and, however white and clear originally, they had taken the deep stains of crimson and gold, the fiery lustre, the black shadow' (91).

The character who is repeatedly associated with Pearl is Mistress Hibbins, who is based upon an actual woman, who, the narrative records, will be accused of witchcraft and who will 'die upon the gallows' (49). In the forest, Dimmesdale likens Pearl's cries to 'the cankered wrath of an old witch, like Mistress Hibbins' (210). Nor can Hester civilize Pearl. Hawthorne suggests that, without a man in the house, Hester is incapable of controlling Pearl's bad behaviour—raising Pearl is described as a process which is identical to an exorcism which Hester is not capable of performing, an attitude towards childrearing that Hawthorne certainly manifested in his journal descriptions in reference to his daughter Una who is described in terms very like those used to describe Pearl: 'The child could not be made amenable to rules', her 'elements were perhaps beautiful and brilliant, but all in disorder' (91).[16]

The process of caring for Pearl, however, leads to Hester's salvation, because through caring for Pearl she avoids becoming a latter-day Anne Hutchinson, and accepts her womanly role, which, according to Hawthorne, is essential if a woman is to be saved. But it is the absent father Dimmesdale who is responsible for Pearl's salvation: as Pearl kisses him at the end of the novel, she feels grief for the first time, and it is this grief, and not her mother's care, which humanizes her:

> Pearl kissed his lips. A spell was broken. The great scene of grief, in which the wild infant bore a part, had developed all her sympathies; and as her tears fell upon her father's cheek, they were the pledge that she would grow up amid human joy and sorrow, nor for ever do battle with the world, but be a woman in it. (256)

This scene effectively obliterates all the years of Hester's mothering. Just as Hawthorne has written his own mother and his wife out of 'The Custom-House', so he writes

Hester out of the cause for Pearl's salvation in *The Scarlet Letter*. It is not all the years of Hester's toil which saves Pearl from a life of evil in Puritan New England, or from being persecuted as a witch, like Mistress Hibbins. Rather, Pearl becomes a happy woman because of this single moment that she shares with her father Dimmesdale which unlocks her ability to feel grief. Salvation comes, not as a result of Pearl and Hester working together through the years to make a reasonably good life for themselves despite persecution. No, salvation comes, in Hawthorne's world, from being humanized as a result of feeling sorry for the suffering your *father* has experienced! And even the reprehensible Chillingworth, in leaving Pearl 'a very considerable amount of property, both here and in England' (261) is made even more responsible for Pearl's good fortune, than all the years of Hester's toil as a single parent, raising her child alone. Hawthorne, therefore, privileges the effect of the absent father upon the good fortune of the child over the labour of the present mother.

It is no wonder, then, that heaven is described in the novel as an all-male paradise, with no room for Hester, a paradise where no women are permitted. Although Hester is buried near Dimmesdale, in paradise, however, in 'the spiritual world, the old physician and the minister—mutual victims as they have been—may ... have found their earthly stock of hatred and antipathy transmuted into golden love' (261).

There has been much feminist critical commentary on *The Scarlet Letter*, which I have summarized in chapters one and two. Frederic I. Carpenter's 'Scarlet A minus' was one of the first critics to point out Hawthorne's ambivalence to his fictional creation, Hester Prynne, and to suggest that critics had overlooked Hawthorne's ambivalent attitude to his literary creation. Carpenter stated that the tendencies in Hawthorne criticism had been to read the novel as if it 'explicitly approves the tragic punishment of Hester's sin and explicitly declares the impossibility of salvation for the sinner' (174); or to state that Hester renounces 'the dead forms of tradition and dared follow the natural laws of her own instinctive nature to the end' (175); or to state how her tragedy 'results . . . from the intrinsic evil of society' (175); or to argue that Hester follows not 'traditional morality, but transcendental truth' (176). According to Carpenter, all those critical stands are inadequate because they do not account for the fact that having 'allowed his imagination to create an idealistic heroine, he did not allow his conscious mind to justify—or even to describe fairly—her ideal morality' (179). Rather, he damned her 'for being romantic and immoral' (179). Hester's greatness as a character, for Carpenter, is not *because of* Hawthorne, who condemned her, but *despite* Hawthorne because she embodies 'the authentic American dream of freedom and independence in the new world' (179).

Morton Cronin in 'Hawthorne on romantic love and the status of women' shares Carpenter's view and believes that 'Hester Prynne is a greater romantic heroine than Hawthorne deserved' (91): 'It is an odd paradox that Hester is perhaps the greatest woman in American fiction because, among other things, her creator did not approve of her.' He cogently observes that part of her appeal is that 'she remains throughout her ordeal unflinchingly devoted to Dimmesdale—for whom every male reader substitutes himself' (91).

Nina Baym's 'The Romantic *malgré lui*' is one of many critical pieces which sees the novel as autobiography. She focuses upon the importance of Hawthorne's 'discovery' of the scarlet A in the Custom-House; she reads 'The Custom-House' as 'psychological autobiography' (14) and sees the novel as 'an autobiographical event' (16) in which Hawthorne openly condemns his ancestors. For Baym, the novel upholds those moral systems which suppress self-expressive acts, which are 'disruptive, and destructive of authority' (21). David Stouck in 'The Surveyor of The Custom-House' also considers the novel autobiographical, and sees 'The Custom-House' as expressing Hawthorne's deep-seated, perhaps unacknowledged, need to return to Salem, 'to the scene of childhood, of putting right the past before living meaningfully in the present' (317). Stouck believes that Hawthorne takes his revenge upon his forebears 'for the sense of unworthiness' (319) they evoked in him, and that he 'idealized the qualities of these paternal figures' (322), and that in writing the work, he 'placated the ghosts of his past' (326). Stouck states that we must view the novel 'as a story about isolation whose characters are symbolic, dream-like projections of the author's alienated state of mind' (329).

Nina Baym's 'Hawthorne and his mother', Gloria Erlich's *Family Themes and Hawthorne's Fiction*, and John Franzosa's '"The Custom-House," *The Scarlet Letter*, and Hawthorne's separation from Salem' see the novel as inspired by, and attempting to come to terms with, the significant loss Hawthorne experienced when his mother died. Baym, as I have stated in chapter two, reads Hester as fictive analogue for Hawthorne's mother; Erlich argues that Hawthorne's mother's death freed him to write his masterpiece; Franzosa states that the novel allowed Hawthorne 'to articulate the "basic fault" in a particular maternal relationship, and to frame a profound self-discovery' (60), that, although 'the fathers are absent, their phallic qualities remain present' and the novel represents 'a search through a maternal configuration for a lost paternal ancestor' (61).

A number of important critical works see the novel in the context of Puritan America. Among them, M. J. Colacurcio's 'Footsteps of Ann Hutchinson' reads the novel against the historical context of the antinomian controversy that prevailed in the colonies and states that '*The Scarlet Letter* is about the reasons why "the woman" Hester Prynne reaches certain antinomian conclusions not unlike those of Ann Hutchinson; and why . . . both the tale and the teller force her to abandon those conclusions' (480). Rather than stating that Hawthorne argues in favour of Hester's actions, Colacurcio states that Hawthorne regards female sexual power as 'a source and type of individualistic nullification of social restraint' (485) and this is one of the major reasons that she is persecuted.

Frederick Newberry sees the historical context of the

novel in a very different way: in 'Tradition and disinheritance in *The Scarlet Letter*', he states that the novel is about the 'conflict between dominant and recessive characteristics of Puritanism and the resolution of the conflict in 1649' (1). In writing the novel, Newberry argues that Hawthorne 'dramatizes the mitigating alternative to the Puritans' militancy, persecution, and iconoclasm' and that it reflects 'the religious tensions between Anglicans and Puritans and the political tensions between the monarchy and Parliament [which] reached a breaking point between 1642 and 1649' (4).

Michael Davitt Bell's *Hawthorne and the Historical Romance of New England* develops the thesis that the 'nineteenth-century romancers' portraits of the founders are of little value to the student of seventeenth-century history. But they are of great value to the student of nineteenth-century literature' (23). For Bell, the great theme which preoccupied writers like Hawthorne was 'the conflict within Puritanism itself between the forces of tyranny and the forces of liberty' (34). And rather than condemning them, Bell states that Hawthorne had 'a balanced view of his forebears' (107). In 'Hawthorne's historical fiction the creation of tragedy, even individual tragedy, is very much a matter of history' (112). Similarly, Nina Baym's 'Passion and authority in *The Scarlet Letter*' discusses 'the conflict between forces of passion and of repression in the psyche and in society' (209) as being one of the main themes of the novel. According to Baym, Hawthorne's representation of the Puritans is historically inaccurate: 'in *The Scarlet Letter* Hawthorne has created an authoritarian state with a Victorian moral outlook' (214).

For those who wish to read the novel as autobiographical, or as historical, Vernon Loggins, *The Hawthornes*, is absolutely indispensable for its history of the family; of William Hathorne, who 'rejoiced when he saw a victim under punishment' (27), who thanked God when Mrs Hutchinson's enemies 'triumphed and sentenced her to banishment' (33), who by '1644 . . . was becoming the most dreaded personage in Essex County' (41); of his son John, who was responsible for the preliminary hearings in the witchcraft trials (131). Loggins recounts the fact, that, following in his ancestor's footsteps, on a school excursion when he was a boy, Nathaniel accused an old woman he knew, and who had been kind enough to give him and his friends a drink, of being a witch:

> repeating what he had read in Hutchinson's *History*, he told how witches ... got control of those they wished to harm. As he went on he kept repeating, 'They always begin by giving a victim witches' broth'. The boys, ... became intent—and then alarmed. Finally they all agreed, 'The tea she gave us *did* have a strange taste!' (228)

In 'The Custom-House', when Hawthorne picks up Hester's scarlet A and places it on his breast, he 'experienced a sensation not altogether physical, yet almost so, as of burning heat; and as if the letter were not of red cloth, but red-hot iron', he 'shuddered, and involuntarily let it fall upon the floor' (32). Although branding was, in fact, a rather typical Puritan punishment for transgressors, it is important to note that Hawthorne records the branding as having occurred (symbolically) to himself, and not to Hester, which serves to focus attention upon himself, and to deflect attention away from her. As she is an adulteress, he becomes an adulterator, as he misleads his audience into thinking that his Puritan forebears were simply intolerant men, rather than sadistic persecutors who repeatedly sentenced adulteresses either to banishment (which meant certain death) or to 'thirty stripes from a knotted whip',[17] which usually led to festering wounds, serious infection, and a long, lingering, painful illness, often resulting in death. Hawthorne has therefore used the novel to control his own past, to rewrite his past into a version that would provide him with less virulent male ancestors and that would present them to the world as less sadistic than they in fact were. And Hawthorne's desire in writing *The Scarlet Letter*, to remove the curse from his Puritan forebears 'now and henceforth' (10) was so immensely successful that his rewritten, highly inaccurate version of Puritan history, which blunts the reality of the persecutions of the time, is the version that most Americans believe, because most Americans learn their Puritan history, not through a history which graphically describes the savagery of the Hathornes, but instead, through reading *The Scarlet Letter*. *The Scarlet Letter* has, indeed, absolved Hawthorne's forebears from guilt, 'now and henceforth'.

CHAPTER FIVE

The House of the Seven Gables (1851)

When Nathaniel Hawthorne sat down to write *The House of the Seven Gables* in September of 1850,[1] the circumstances of his life had changed considerably since the publication of *The Scarlet Letter* some six months before.[2] Hawthorne wrote to his friend Horatio Bridge, that he was now enjoying the fruits of his efforts: 'First, the pleasurable toil of writing; second, the gratification of one's family and friends; and, lastly, the solid cash.'[3] For the first time in his literary career, Hawthorne was famous, with five thousand copies of *The Scarlet Letter* in print,[4] and reviews, like that of E. P. Whipple, proclaiming that the novel was filled with 'tragic interest and tragic power', and that it was 'deep in thought' and 'condensed in style'. And he now had the firm support of a publisher who encouraged him to write: James T. Fields (of Ticknor, Reed & Fields), pleased with the success of *The Scarlet Letter*, had written 'We intend to publish your books à-la-Steam Engine.'[5]

Before Hawthorne began the novel, the Hawthornes had moved from Salem into a farmhouse in Lenox, Massachusetts, in the Berkshires, close to a colony of artists, writers and reformers which included Catherine Maria Sedgwick and Oliver Wendell Holmes. On 5 August Hawthorne was the honoured guest of Herman Melville, who, like Hawthorne, was at the height of his literary powers, writing *Moby Dick*, which was to change dramatically as a result of this meeting and the impact of Hawthorne's work upon Melville's style. Soon after, Melville anonymously published 'Hawthorne and his Mosses', in *Literary World*, in which he favourably compared Hawthorne with Shakespeare, separating him from the sentimental writers of his day because of his courage in drawing upon 'the dark half' of his soul, which heightened his reputation still further.[6]

In his preface to *The Scarlet Letter*, Hawthorne had predicted that, although he knew he would leave Salem—and he left amidst the rancour and bitterness that was caused by the savage portraits of his compatriots in 'The Custom-House'—'my old native town will loom upon me through the haze of memory, . . . as if it were no portion of the real earth, but an overgrown village in cloud-land, with only imaginary inhabitants to people its wooden houses, and walk its homely lanes'.[7] Hawthorne composed his portrait of the Pyncheons, a Salem family, with roots as deep in Salem's soil as Hawthorne's own, in his upstairs study in the small red farmhouse in Lenox. The novel was composed quickly—Hawthorne took but five months to complete it—yet there are indications in his correspondence that the work did not proceed as easily as the writing of *The Scarlet Letter*. Although, at first, Hawthorne believed that the subject was 'more characteristic of my mind, and more proper and natural for me to write, than "The Scarlet Letter"',[8] he later wrote, 'the book requires more care and thought than the "Scarlet Letter";—also, I have to wait oftener for a mood'.[9]

One of Hawthorne's problems was the ending of the novel. The subject of *The House of the Seven Gables* is the continuing effect of the curse which Matthew Maule pronounces upon the Pyncheon family when he is wrongly condemned to death for being a wizard—a charge which Colonel Pyncheon has trumped up to get his land—yet the novel ends happily, with a reconciliation between the families effected by the marriage between Phoebe (a Pyncheon) and Holgrave (a Maule). The ending might have been a concession to public taste; or it might have been written with his wife Sophia in mind, to exalt the power of love to change the world: Hawthorne has used the name Phoebe—one of his pet names for his wife Sophia—for the name of his central female character, and it is inconceivable that he would let that character come to any harm in the novel. To many critics, the ending seems contrived, rather than an organic outgrowth of the novel, and Hawthorne himself saw the problem: 'in writing it, I suppose I was illuminated by my purpose to bring it to a prosperous close; while the gloom of the past threw its shadow along the reader's pathway.'[10]

Another of Hawthorne's problems was that he was, once again, dredging up some very troublesome autobiographical material—his family's involvement in the Salem witchcraft trails; his suppressed rage at his Uncle Robert Manning, which was transferred onto the character of Judge Pyncheon; his ambivalent concern for the welfare of his spinster sisters, Elizabeth and Louisa, who had been entrusted to his care by his mother on her deathbed, when she entreated him 'to take care of my sisters'; and his continued exasperation with Elizabeth Peabody[11] (all three provided models for his portrait of the spinster Hepzibah); and his incestuous feelings for his sister Elizabeth, which are represented by Hepzibah's preoccupation with her brother Clifford.

In the novel, Hawthorne explores the effect of the acts of one's ancestors upon one's own life: 'the little regarded truth, that the act of the passing generation is the germ which may and must produce good or evil fruit, in a far distant time' (6). This appears to be a very different stance from 'The Custom-House', where Hawthorne stated his intention to exonerate his ancestors; here he states that the evil deeds of one's ancestors cannot be so easily dismissed, that they may, in fact, 'include a chain of events, extending over the better part of two centuries' (5). And yet, the end of the novel nullifies that insight because all ends well—Judge Pyncheon's death provides enough money for Clifford, Hepzibah, Holgrave, and Phoebe to live in the country without ever having to work again, and the spell of the past is broken because Phoebe and Holgrave fall in love.

The fictional Pyncheon family is directly analogous to

the Hawthorne family, and Hawthorne uses, as a central ingredient of his plot, the very curse which legend held had been pronounced against a member of his own family as a result of their persecution of witches. At the beginning of *The House of the Seven Gables*, Matthew Maule, about to be executed, utters the curse upon Colonel Pyncheon, 'God will give him blood to drink!' (8); legend held that, during the Salem witchcraft trials, one of the accused, Rebecca Nurse, had pointed to Judge Hathorne, saying 'You're a liar! I'm no more a witch than you're a wizard! And if you take my life God will give you blood to drink!'[12]

Hawthorne has taken the legend which was an intimate part of his life, and changed the gender of the person who is being persecuted for witchcraft, and the person who pronounces the curse, from female to male. This is a very important, and misleading change. By inventing the character of Matthew Maule, Hawthorne shifts the legend from being woman-centred to being man-centred. Moreover, Hawthorne, by focusing on the persecution of wizards, and eliminating the persecution of witches, effectively obliterates from his version of the legend all of those *women* who were persecuted for witchcraft in Puritan New England.

Throughout the history of the persecution of witches, the 'ratio of women to men executed has been variously estimated at 20 to 1 and 100 to 1'. In Puritan New England, wizards as well as witches were persecuted, although there were significantly more women killed than men. As Andrea Dworkin has remarked, 'Witchcraft was a woman's crime.'[13] By changing the woman accused of witchcraft who pronounces the curse into a man accused of being a wizard, Hawthorne is denying women readers of his romance a moment of their history. In rewriting the legend, Hawthorne also diminishes the power of women, because, in his version, the terror and vengeance of the curse, intimately associated with the woman who pronounces it, is now associated with a man. In transforming the curse from a woman's curse to a man's curse, Hawthorne effectively expunges from the universe of his fiction the possibility that a woman can be vengeful if she has been wrongly persecuted. In Hawthorne's fiction, it is the wronged *man* who becomes feared, and the images of vengeance and violence in the novel are rendered in completely male terms.

Hawthorne presents the persecution of Maule (and the witchcraft phenomenon in general) as linked to an attempt to acquire property on the part of an avaricious high-ranking Puritan: Colonel Pyncheon accuses the humble Matthew Maule, builder of 'a hut, shaggy with thatch' (6), of wizardry in order to get his property. In fact, as Paul Boyer and Stephen Nissenbaum have observed, whereas the first three women accused as witches were outsiders (a slave, a beggar, an elderly woman), those men who were accused of being wizards tended to be *high*-ranking—a minister, a shipowner, two selectmen of Salem town, several men with estates in Boston, a wealthy Boston merchant, one of the judges of the witchcraft court: 'the overall direction of the accusations remains clear: up the social ladder, fitfully but perceptibly, to its very top'.[14] If Hawthorne wished to represent the history of wizardry accurately, *Matthew Maule* would have accused Colonel Pyncheon, for a variety of complex reasons defined by Boyer and Nissenbaum, among them, an unconscious envy on the part of the less affluent members of Puritan Salem towards those wealthier Salemites who were becoming more mercantile than Puritan.

Although Hawthorne describes the 'indiscrimination with which they persecuted, not merely the poor and the aged, . . . but people of all ranks; their own equals, brethren, and wives' (8), 'none of these persons of quality was ever brought to trial, much less executed'.[15] It is significant that Hawthorne places women at the end of his list, that it is the least important category, that he implies, through the words 'people', 'equals', and 'brethren', that there were many more male victims than female victims, and that he does not even mention unmarried women, or beggar women, or the toddler girl, Dorcas Good, who was accused of being a witch when she was four years old, and spent nine months in heavy irons.[16]

Hawthorne describes the witchcraft trials, in one place,

as a 'passionate error' (8), yet in another as 'an unfortunate overdoing of a work praiseworthy in itself' (188). According to the critic Morton Cronin, Hawthorne possessed within himself the vengeance of his forebears: 'Unlike his judicial ancestor, who consigned a witch to the gallows with an undismayed countenance, Hawthorne would have sprung the trap with a sigh.'[17]

Early in the novel, Hawthorne describes the witchcraft trials in the following terms:

> Old Matthew Maule . . . was executed for the crime of witchcraft. He was one of the martyrs to that terrible delusion which should teach us, among its other morals, that the influential classes, and those who take upon themselves to be leaders of the people, are fully liable to all the passionate error that has ever characterized the maddest mob. Clergymen, judges, statesmen—the wisest, calmest, holiest persons of their day—stood in the inner circle roundabout the gallows, loudest to applaud the work of blood, latest to confess themselves miserably deceived. (7–8)

There is no mention in Hawthorne's account of John Hathorne's role in the witchcraft proceedings, and Hawthorne makes it appear as if the inhabitants of Salem were unanimous in their persecution of witches.

As early as 1831, an important political enemy of Hawthorne's during the dispute which led to his leaving the Custom-House post,[18] Charles Wentworth Upham, the foremost nineteenth-century authority on the trials, had been circulating a very different version of that period in Salem's history than the version Hawthorne told in *The House of the Seven Gables*. According to Upham, and his very careful analysis of the transcriptions of the trials (which he presents in his volume), John Hathorne was largely responsible for the excesses of that period.[19] In a series of damning statements, Upham demonstrated how Hathorne manipulated evidence, and lied to the accused, in order to elicit admissions of guilt. In writing of the examination of Sarah Good, for example, Upham wrote: 'It will be noticed that the examination was conducted in the form of questions put by the magistrate, Hathorne, based upon a foregone conclusion of the prisoner's guilt. . . . Altogether, the proceedings against her, which terminated with her execution, were cruel and shameful to the highest degree.'[20] Upham was clear: the villain of the Salem witchcraft trials was John Hathorne; the man responsible for the execution of innocent people was John Hathorne. And Hathorne's conduct, Upham proved, could not be explained away as an error based upon the theology of the times, because Upham documented how Hathorne deliberately falsified evidence. Nor could it be held that Hathorne merely represented the view of other Salemites, for Upham documented how other Salem inhabitants, including Hathorne's own sister, Elizabeth Porter, tried to stop the trials.[21]

Hawthorne depicts the history of the times very differently, and, of course, very self-servingly, for there is no John Hathorne in evidence in *The House of the Seven Gables* who is held up for censure. Hawthorne must have been aware of Upham's interpretation of his ancestor's role in the trials, and, in one sense, this reader sees the novel as an attempt to put forward a view of the witchcraft trials that is very different from the one that Upham was promulgating. And Hawthorne's strategy, if one may call it that, was successful. By centring the attention of the text on the curse that is uttered, rather than on the persecution of witches, and his ancestor's role in the persecution, Hawthorne deflects attention away from John Hathorne and counters Upham's view as well. In one very important sense, the novel can be thought of as an attempt to impress upon the reader's imagination a view which would act as antidote to Upham's damning portrait.

After the Custom-House episode, Hawthorne had expressed his hatred and desire for vengeance against Upham: 'I shall do my best to kill and scalp him in the public prints; and I think I shall succeed.'[22] James R. Mellow, Hawthorne's biographer, points out that the character of Judge Pyncheon is a deliberately negative portrait of Upham: in 'sketching out the hypocritical character of the judge . . . Hawthorne undoubtedly intended to point a finger at his old political enemy, the smiling and unctuous Charles Wentworth Upham'.[23] Not only is the novel, therefore, an attempt to supplant Upham's view of the trials with Hawthorne's own; the novel also contains a character assassination of the man promulgating those views, which would surely render them suspect.

Hawthorne turns his attention, in chapters II, III, and IV of the novel, to the character of Hepzibah Pyncheon, an elderly spinster, who, for the first time in her life, is forced to earn her own living: 'Poverty, treading closely at her heels for a lifetime, has come up with her at last. She must earn her own food, or starve!' (38). Hepzibah, who is referred to as 'the old maid',[24] is 'wretchedly poor' (24), on the threshold of utter destitution. She decides to open a shop, which is 'almost the only resource of women, in circumstances at all similar to those of our unfortunate recluse' (38).

The narrator describes Hepzibah's poverty as if it is her fault: she 'seemed to make it [her poverty] her choice to remain so; inasmuch as her affluent cousin, the Judge had repeatedly offered her all the comforts of life' (24). The other alternative open to her, besides petty employment, is to place herself at the mercy of a male relative. The narrator does not reveal, however, that Hepzibah's choice to risk penury rather than to take Judge Pyncheon's largesse is the result of her loyalty to her brother, Clifford, whom the Judge has sent off to jail. In fact, *The House of the Seven Gables* accurately delineates the only ways in which women in the nineteenth century could support themselves, and the dependence of many women upon the generosity of the male members of their family, which had been the fate of Hawthorne's mother and his sisters.

But in the novel, Hawthorne misrepresents Hepzibah's fate as if it were a class issue, rather than a gender issue, by describing what has happened to her as if it is the proper and fitting come-uppance of a member of the privileged class, who has chosen not to work, and whose fortune has now taken a turn for the worse:

> It was the final term of what called itself old gentility. A lady—who had fed herself from childhood with the shadowy food of aristocratic reminiscences, and whose religion it was, that a lady's hand soils itself irremediably by doing aught for bread—this born lady, after sixty years of narrowing means, is fain to step down from her pedestal of imaginary rank. . . . And we have stolen upon Miss Hepzibah Pyncheon, . . . at the instant of time when the patrician lady is to be transformed into the plebian woman. (37–8)

Using Hepzibah to signify the decline of the Pyncheon fortunes (which is described as the working out of the Maule curse against the Pyncheons) elides the fact that a woman of Hepzibah's class could not work even if she chose to, and could not own property in any event; it was not a lady's 'religion', as the narrator describes it, that her hand should not soil itself 'irremediably by doing aught for bread' but, rather, a matter of social and public policy. To describe Hepzibah, or any female member of this class, as having *chosen* not to work is to misrepresent the facts of history and the locus of economic power: in fact, a woman in Hepzibah's position had virtually no choice but to become a lady.

The narrator describes Hepzibah's preparation for her first day of work: Hepzibah begins 'what it would be mockery to term the adornment of her person' (30); but no matter how much time she spends trying to adorn herself, she will be unsuccessful; 'when she shall have done her utmost' to effect 'the matitutinal repair and beautifying of an elderly person', 'it were the best charity to turn one's eyes another way' (31); she opens bureau drawers with 'spasmodic jerks'; she closes them with 'fidgety reluctance' (31); she crosses the room on tiptoe, which is 'the customary gait of elderly women' (36).

Despite the narrator's ostensible acknowledgement of the perilous nature of Hepzibah's position, that she is on the brink of starvation, the tone of the description is hostile. Rather than recognizing that Hepzibah's position is a desperate one, the language used to describe Hepzibah reduces her to a figure of mockery, and the word used most often to describe her attempt to save herself from the poorhouse is the word 'ludicrous': he describes how 'a deeply tragic character . . . contrasted irreconcilably with the ludicrous pettiness of her employment' (37); how it 'is a heavy annoyance to a writer . . . that so much of the mean and ludicrous should be hopelessly mixed up with the purest pathos which life anywhere supplies to him' (40–1). Moreover, the narrator asks the reader's permission to see Hepzibah as a figure of fun, and so subtly includes the reader in the process of excoriating her: 'Heaven help our poor old Hepzibah, and forgive us for taking a ludicrous view of her position!'(37).

The consequence of Hepzibah's having lived the life of a lady is that she believes herself to be utterly incapable of functioning in the world: 'for above a quarter of a century gone-by, [Hepzibah] has dwelt in strict seclusion; taking no part in the business of life, and just as little in its intercourse and pleasures' (31). And so Hepzibah's first foray into the mercantile world is terrifying and Hepzibah anticipates the likelihood of her own failure: 'How could the born lady—the recluse of half-a-lifetime, utterly unpractised in the world, at sixty years of age—how could she ever dream of succeeding' (48). Yet the moment that she earns her first copper, she has the exhilarating rush of the possibilities that are now open to her, even though she might be incapable of realizing them. She feels 'a thrill of almost youthful enjoyment' (51); she feels a surge of power: 'So miraculous the strength that we do not know of! The healthiest glow, that Hepzibah had known for years, had come now, . . . when, for the first time, she had put forth her hand to help herself' (52).

Hepzibah's new position as a wage-earner permits her to look afresh at the class system. Before now, she had disparaged 'the temper and manners of what she termed the lower classes, whom . . . she had looked down upon with a gentle and pitying complacence, as herself occupying a sphere of unquestionable superiority' (55). Now, however, she possesses 'a sentiment of virulence . . . towards the idle aristocracy to which it had so recently been her pride to belong' (55). And the narrator states that *work* is the distinguishing factor between being a lady, which implies 'not privilege, but restriction' and being a 'true woman' (45). But the novel does not support this contention because even as Hepzibah toils she hopes that 'some harlequin-trick of fortune' (64) will save her, and when it comes, in the form of an inheritance, she quickly abandons her work to become a member of the landed gentry.

Hepzibah has remained secluded for all these years because of her maidenhood, and also her utter devotion (or enslavement) to her brother. Hepzibah takes a miniature from a writing desk 'representing . . . the likeness of a young man, in a silken dressing-gown of an old fashion, . . . with its full, tender lips, and beautiful eyes, that seem to indicate not so much capacity of thought, as gentle and voluptuous emotion' (31–2). The similarity between this description and Hawthorne's portraits is striking. Hepzibah gazes at it with the rapture of a lover, and there is surely an incestuous quality to the intensity of her devotion: 'Can it have been an early lover of Miss Hepzibah? No; she never had a lover—poor thing, how could she?' (32). She couldn't because the nature of her love for Clifford would not allow it.

Clifford, however, returns her devotion by despising the very sight of her. Although the narrator locates the source of Clifford's disgust in his highly developed aesthetic sensibility, it is clear that Clifford can only tolerate the sight of women who are young and pretty, like Phoebe: the sight of mature female flesh nauseates him, although the sight of his elderly male flesh does not elicit these feelings of revulsion in either Hepzibah or Phoebe. Phoebe, when she looks at his wasted frame, detects a glimmer of the old beauty: 'There had been something so innately characteristic in this look, that all the dusky years . . . did not suffice utterly to destroy it' (106). Clifford, however, cannot look at Hepzibah and 'It was Hepzibah's misfortune; not Clifford's fault. How could he—so yellow as she was, so wrinkled, so sad of mien, with that odd uncouthness of a turban on her head, and that most perverse of scowls contorting her brow—how could he love to gaze at her!' (109). In one important sense, Hepzibah has been victimized by her love for Clifford; her overwhelming love for him has prevented her from establishing a life for herself beyond him; her love for him has controlled her life and taken on the contours of an unrequited love affair: she 'felt a reverence for the pictured visage [of Clifford], of which only a far-descended and time-stricken virgin could be susceptible' (34).

Hawthorne thus explicates how a woman can be victimized as a result of loving too ardently; Hepzibah asked nothing in life 'but the opportunity of devoting herself to this brother whom she had so loved' (133). Moreover, he defines how the lifelong love and services of a maiden can be secured by a household in which incestuous love is encouraged. Indeed, both Clifford and Hepzibah presume that it is her responsibility to support him—'you must know, dearest Clifford, that we are very poor. And there was no resource, but . . . to earn our subsistence with my own hands!' (113)—even if he acts despicably to her, and reviles her for her attempt to work.

Phoebe, the seventeen-year-old cousin of the Pyncheons, who comes to Salem from the country, is in precisely the same position as Hepzibah, although there is no recognition of this in the novel. Phoebe has been cast out of her own household as a result of her mother's second marriage: 'which made it desirable for Phoebe to establish herself in another home' (73). The reason why it is now desirable for Phoebe to establish herself elsewhere remains unuttered. None the less, what is striking about Phoebe's fate is that, for whatever reasons, Phoebe's mother does not have the power or the will to see to it that her daughter is cared for. She is thus set adrift, and winds up on Hepzibah's doorstep, who initially responds 'I really can't see my way clear to keep you with me' (73), for Phoebe is simply another mouth to feed, and Hepzibah is having difficulty enough feeding herself.

Underneath her guise of innocence, Phoebe is clever, and she states that she has 'no idea of forcing herself on her cousin's protection', that she will merely visit for 'a week or two'. Phoebe understands that she must ingratiate herself into this household, or she will be at tremendous risk, and so she tells Hepzibah 'I mean to earn my bread' (74).

What ensues in the household is an illuminating exploration of the way in which women of privilege, like Hepzibah, rely upon women like Phoebe to do their work for them. Phoebe soon takes over all the household tasks, from cooking and cleaning to tending the garden—all of which are beyond Hepzibah's capacities, and soon begins to run the shop as well. There is no recognition, however, either on Hepzibah's part, or on the narrator's, that this work requires effort and energy, that it is unpaid, and that it is sheer drudgery: 'Whatever she did, too, was done without conscious effort, and with frequent outbreaks of song which were exceedingly pleasant to the ear. . . . It betokened the cheeriness of an active temperament, finding joy in its activity, and therefore rendering it beautiful . . .' (76). Hawthorne here writes of the romance of housework. He suggests that a woman can only accomplish her housework easily if her moral fibre is correct: Phoebe has 'the purifying influence . . . of one, youthful, fresh, and thoroughly wholesome heart' (137); she possesses the 'magnetism of innate fitness' (76). 'These things are not to be learnt; they depend upon a knack that comes . . . with one's mother's blood' (78). Conversely, any woman (like Hepzibah), who complains about this work or who can't do it must be suspect—a view about women and housework that lingers to this day. *The House of the Seven Gables* can thus be read as the forerunner of American television commercials in which women sing and smile as they scrub floors and wash their husbands' shirts. And, just as in those commercials, what Hawthorne covertly sells in his novel is the notion that the very fabric of civilization depends upon there being an angel-woman like Phoebe in the house to minister to the physical well-being of its inhabitants: because of her very presence, 'the gnawing tooth of the dry-rot was stayed, the dust had ceased to settle down so densely from the antique ceilings' (136). And this is not how things are but, rather, how things should (and must) be: 'it should be woman's office to move in the midst of practical affairs, and to gild them all— the very homeliest, were it even the scouring of pots and kettles—with an atmosphere of loveliness and joy' (80).

Writing the myth of the angel in the house entails mystifying housework and investing it with a sacral quality: the 'vapor of the broiled fish arose like incense'; 'Indian cakes were the sweetest offering of all . . . , befitting the rustic altars of the innocent and golden age'; and hand-churned butter is 'a propitiatory gift' (100–1). Inherent in this mythology is the idea that only women are capable of performing these sacred and mysterious rites: 'What was precisely Phoebe's process, we find it impossible to say' (72). Writing the romance of housework also entails redefining women's work as non-work, which justifies not paying her for it, or, even worse, as play, which suggests that she should be grateful to have the opportunity to do it:[25]

> The life of the long and busy day—spent in occupations that might so easily have taken a squalid and ugly aspect—had been made pleasant, and even lovely, by the spontaneous grace with which these homely duties seemed to bloom out of her character; so that labour, while she dealt with it, had the easy and flexible charm of play. Angels do not toil, but let their good works grow out of them; and so did Phoebe. (82)

Hawthorne's narrative obscures the fact that Phoebe, like the Italian boy with the monkey and the hurdy-gurdy, who appears periodically in the novel, is, quite literally, singing for her supper, and that she must act the part of the naive innocent angel because Hepzibah's continuing tolerance of her presence depends upon her constant work coupled with her appearance of utter insouciance. What the narrative obscures is the fact that Phoebe's posture as the angel in the house is her strategy to keep from starving.

But Hawthorne renders the reality differently. Phoebe turns the decrepit mansion into Eden, and plays Eve to Clifford's 'thunder-smitten Adam' (150). When he returns from prison, the presence of Phoebe is sufficient to bring him back to life: her presence 'transfigured him with an expression that could only be interpreted as the glow of an exquisite and happy spirit' (139). Hawthorne expresses here the nineteenth-century view that the moral fibre of the men of a family depend, not upon their own actions, but upon the presence of innately good women. Clifford

> took unfailing note of every charm that appertained to her sex, and saw the ripeness of her lips, and the virginal development of her bosom. All her little, womanly ways, budding out of her like blossoms on a young fruit-tree, had their effect on him, and sometimes caused his very heart to tingle with the keenest thrills of pleasure. (141)

Not only is Phoebe completely responsible for cooking, cleaning, and running the store, but she has become the keeper of Clifford's soul; she has become utterly responsible for Clifford's emotional and moral well-being. But he does not understand, nor does the narrator recognize, that she is a person with needs too—she gives love to him 'because he needed so much love' (143); but he does not give her any love. Nor does he recognize that she is a human being: rather, she is 'a bird' (138), a fruit, 'a flower' (143), 'a prayer' (168): 'She was not an actual fact for him, but the interpretation of all that he had lacked on earth'; throughout, she remains 'mere symbol' (142).

Hawthorne here describes the angel in the house, the attitude about women which contemporary feminists criticize: that women should be the source of all comfort, while the myth prevails that women, themselves, do not require comfort, and should not ask for it, for it is in their nature to give and not to receive. Indeed Clifford's treatment of Hepzibah and Phoebe are flip sides of the same misogynist coin: whether he loathes or adores, he denies them the status of persons with needs that he can fulfil; he cannot see them other than caring for him.

Holgrave, the reformer,[26] descendant of the Maules (although no one is at first aware of his lineage), lives in the Pyncheon household and comes into contact with Phoebe. He is suspicious of all institutions, and hopes to tear down the 'moss-grown and rotten Past' 'and everything to begin anew' (179). He despises the idea of ancestry, and thinks that 'once in every half-century, at longest, a family should be merged into the great, obscure mass of humanity, and forget all about its ancestors' (185). But, like Clifford, Holgrave is solipsistic and egomaniacal: while he describes his plans for a new and better world, 'he forgot Phoebe while he talked to her' (182), and, of course, never consults her about what she believes the future state of the world might look like, probably because he believes that he 'could read her off like a page of a child's story-book' (182).

Early in his relationship with Phoebe, Holgrave reads her 'Alice Pyncheon', his version of a legend describing the vengeance undertaken by Gervayse Pyncheon, the grandson of Matthew Maule, against the Pyncheon family, which he wishes to publish. The tale describes how Gervayse's retaliation against the Pyncheons consists of destroying the life of Alice Pyncheon, even though Alice has had nothing to do with her grandfather's behaviour: 'Alice Pyncheon', the story within the novel which Holgrave has composed, reveals his deep-seated belief that the way you get even for the sins of the fathers is to make a victim out of the fathers' women.

Thus Gervayse seeks to mesmerize Alice, so that he can control her, and he asks her to 'fix your eyes on mine!' (203). The narrator describes Pyncheon's attempt to gain power over Alice as if it were a contest between the power of the male and the power of the female:

> this fair girl deemed herself conscious of a power—combined of beauty, high, unsullied purity, and the preservative force of womanhood—that could make her sphere impenetrable. . . . She instinctively knew . . . that some sinister or evil potency was now striving to pass her barriers; nor would she decline the contest. So Alice put woman's might against man's might; a match not often equal, on the part of woman. (203)

The narrator's language here suggests that Alice will weather Gervayse's assault only if she is pure: this duplicates the assumption underpinning the testing of witches—if the woman was pure she would endure the test, no matter what the test was. Indeed, Alice is likened to a witch:

her presence in the Pyncheon household imparted a 'faint witchery to the whole edifice' (191). Elsewhere, the narrator implies that Alice deserves whatever punishment Pyncheon might concoct for her, because she is proud and arrogant: 'a man of generous nature would have forgiven all her pride. . . . All that he would have required, was simply the acknowledgement that he was indeed a man, and a fellow-being, moulded of the same elements as she' (201).

And so, it is suggested that Alice deserves what she gets. She becomes Gervayse's property, and,

> while Alice Pyncheon lived, she was Maule's slave, in a bondage more humiliating, a thousand-fold, than that which binds its chains around the body. Seated by his humble fireside, Maule had but to wave his hand; and, wherever the proud lady chanced to be . . . , her spirit passed from beneath her own control, and bowed itself to Maule. (208–9)

It is clear, of course, that Holgrave's attitude and Gervayse's are identical, and one wonders why Phoebe is later willing to marry Holgrave when his story so obviously demonstrates a pathological wish to murder a Pyncheon woman in order to get his revenge.

Phoebe's love for Holgrave is described as an act of self-annihilation; now that she loves him, she has a 'veil . . . muffled about her, in which she could behold only him, and live only in his thoughts and emotions' (211). He believes that with

> one wave of his hand and a corresponding effort of his will, he could complete his mastery over Phoebe's yet free and virgin spirit; he could establish an influence over this good, pure, and simple child, as dangerous, and perhaps as disastrous, as that which [Gervayse] . . . had acquired and exercised over the ill-fated Alice. (212)

But the narrator assures us that Holgrave possesses 'the rare and high quality of reverence for another's individuality' which prevented him from twisting 'that one link more, which might have rendered his spell over Phoebe indissoluble'

(212), and the narrator suggests that their love conquers all and negates the negative effects of the age-old curse.

Several Hawthorne critics share the narrator's belief that the end of the novel demonstrates the redemptive power of love. Jerome Klinkowitz, in 'Hawthorne's sense of an ending', points out that 'love . . . is in fact a resolution' (43) in each of his romances; David W. Pancost, in 'Hawthorne's epistemology and ontology' also believes that Phoebe's and Holgrave's love 'promises to create an Edenic reality' (12).

William B. Dillingham's 'Structure and theme in *The House of the Seven Gables*' also reads the end of the novel as optimistic in that it demonstrates Hawthorne's belief in 'what Holgrave terms "the united struggle of mankind"'; throughout the novel, 'the desirability of a democratic way of life over an aristocratic one' (60), the desirability of an 'unisolated' life over 'psychological isolation', and 'the dichotomy between appearance and reality' (60–1) further the theme.

The feminist critic Nina Baym concurs in reading the end of the novel as positive.[27] Baym reads *The House of the Seven Gables* as a demonstration of the idea that 'the seen present is controlled by the unseen past' (154), and as a further working out of the theme in *The Scarlet Letter*, of 'the romantic conflict . . . between forces of passion, spontaneity, and creativity and counterforces of regulation and control' (154–5), 'embodied respectively in Maule and Pyncheon' (155). According to Baym, the novel explores several antagonisms, 'aristocrat versus democrat, conservative versus radical, institutionalist versus transcendentalist', but the most important struggle occurs within the human soul, 'with authority trying to suppress passion and passion to depose authority' (155). In addition, she sees Hawthorne establishing a myth of the origins of civilization as having been founded 'on a crime' which entails the fact that civilized beings are, of necessity 'oppressed, distorted, incomplete' (156).

But Baym believes that Hawthorne approves of Holgrave and 'his radical ideas'; to 'Hawthorne's generally weak male protagonists Holgrave is an exception, in his courage, high principles, ideals, kindheartedness, self-reliance, and sensitivity' (158). Although Baym believes that Alice Pyncheon's story is analogous to the present-day tale, she believes that 'Alice is partly victimized by her self and partly by her father' in his 'greed for possessions' (160), and she also believes that Holgrave's 'refusal to take advantage of the opportunity given him by Phoebe's response demonstrates his moral worth' (162). Holgrave's loving Phoebe, for Baym, is an index of his new, 'complex, stable relations to the social order' (167).

Gloria C. Erlich's feminist-inspired reading in *Family Themes and Hawthorne's Fiction* states that the oppressive paternal figures in the novel are linked both to Hawthorne's Puritan forebears, and to the Mannings as well: 'The portrayal of Judge Pyncheon is a calculated mixture of ancestral Hathorne and contemporary Manning, of cruelty, greed, and hypocritical benevolence, including even attenuated sensibility' (139). And she argues persuasively that both the figure of Clifford and that of Holgrave 'represent phases of response to . . . the . . . embodiment of authoritarian oppression' (141): Clifford has not developed his artistic potential and instead 'develops . . . a somewhat leering voyeurism with respect to Phoebe's developing womanhood' (141); Holgrave's decision to marry Phoebe 'made impulsively . . . , and his entire swing over to conservatism seem a retreat before visionary powers that are simply too dangerous' (142). It is no wonder, therefore, that the 'narrator's response to the open-eyed corpse' is to 'positively gloat over the seated body of the older man' (143).

But Carl Schoen's 'House of the Seven Deadly Sins' suggests that the novel is carefully structured to permit the consequences of a 'particular vice to be displayed prominently' (27); he suggests that Hawthorne uses mesmerism in the novel as a 'symbolic substitute' for sex: 'Hawthorne was concerned with that aspect of sexual attraction which aroused the impulse to dominate and enslave' (31).

In the judgement of this reader, the ending of *The House of the Seven Gables* cannot be read as suggesting an Edenic lifetime for Phoebe. In the novel, the only thing that prevents Phoebe's fate from being exactly like that of Alice Pyncheon is Holgrave's self control. Rather than there being a resolution to the issues in the novel, this reader believes that the novel ends essentially where it begins. Although at the beginning of the novel all of the power rested in the hands of the Pyncheons, and they exercised that power over the Maules, at the end of the novel all the power rests in the hands of Holgrave, and the only thing that stands in the way of his exercising it over Phoebe is his own self-control (not his innate goodness). It is important that all the power, all the control is described as being Holgrave's; Phoebe is powerless to resist should Holgrave choose to control her. This is a stunningly insightful description of the possibility for tyranny within the institution of heterosexual love and marriage: Hawthorne seems to be admitting here that the only thing standing in the way of a woman's victimization in marriage is the choice her husband makes not to victimize the woman who loves him. Thus the possibility for tyranny in marriage becomes equivalent to the actual tyranny of Hawthorne's Puritan ancestor John Hathorne who persecuted witches.

And so, even if Hawthorne's narrator is sanguine about Phoebe's fate, this feminist reader is not. Is one really to believe, as the narrator apparently does, that Holgrave, given his desire to dominate and victimize a woman, so chillingly demonstrated in 'Alice Pyncheon', will control this urge all the days of his life? One fears for Phoebe's life with Holgrave; marriage to him, the feminist reader suspects, might result in a bondage of the spirit similar to Judge Pyncheon's wife who 'got her death-blow in the honey-moon, and never smiled again, because her husband compelled her to serve him' (123).

Indeed, Phoebe herself believes that if she marries Holgrave she will 'sink down, and perish' (306). Coming after this recognition, one can hardly believe the narrator's euphoria as he intones:

> The bliss, which makes all things true, beautiful, and holy, shone around this youth and maiden. They were conscious of nothing sad nor old. They transfigured the earth, and made it Eden again, and themselves the two first dwellers in it. (307)

CHAPTER SIX

The Blithedale Romance (1852)

Nathaniel Hawthorne began *The Blithedale Romance* after the family had moved from Lenox to West Newton, Massachusetts, and settled into the home of Horace and Mary Mann (Sophia's sister).[1] The satire of social reformers is a central focus in *The Blithedale Romance*, and it is not coincidental that Hawthorne wrote the work while ensconced in the Mann household. Horace and Mary Mann worked long and hard both while Mann was a Whig member of Congress, and throughout their lives, to effect many of the reforms which Hawthorne satirizes in the novel: temperance, the treatment of the insane, prison conditions, anti-slavery, and the movement for women's rights.[2] It irked Hawthorne that Sophia's mother much preferred Horace Mann, and Mother Peabody inflamed the rivalry by sending Hawthorne Mann's speeches against Hawthorne's democratic political allies, such as General Pierce and Noah Webster. Mann's and Hawthorne's views had polarized: while Mann put his life at risk to defend Captain Daniel Drayton, who carried fugitive slaves into free territory, Hawthorne wrote, in his biography of Pierce, that 'slavery may be one of those evils which divine Providence does not leave to be remedied by human contrivances, but which, in its own good time . . . it causes to vanish'.[3] It must have given Hawthorne great pleasure to create the portrait of the benighted reformer Hollingsworth, whose schemes to reform society ultimately count for naught, while in the home of Horace Mann.

Hawthorne drew heavily upon his personal experience as a member of the Brook Farm Community at West Roxbury in 1841, and his notebook became a source while he wrote the novel. On 24 July 1851, Nathaniel Hawthorne wrote to William Pike, 'When I write another romance, I shall take the Community for a subject, and shall give some of my experiences and observations at Brook Farm.'[4] One entry, dated 9 October 1841, describes 'a little sempstress from Boston, about seventeen years old', with 'the material for that sober character, a wife',[5] yet who was 'a little vulgar', who became the inspiration for Priscilla. Another entry, dated 28 September 1841, describing 'a company of fantastic figures, arranged in a ring for a dance or game',[6] was drawn upon for chapter XXIV, 'The masqueraders'. Hawthorne's description of how he 'lay under the trees and looked on' at the celebration is identical to the vantage point from which his narrator, Miles Coverdale, relates the scene.

Hawthorne had joined the experimental community in 1841, committing one thousand dollars to the venture,[7] hoping that he could eventually make a home there with Sophia. He was initially euphoric about the possibility of combining dignified manual labour with his writing. On 13 April 1841 he wrote to Sophia: 'I shall make an excellent husbandman. I feel the original Adam reviving within me.'[8] But the idyll didn't last. By 28 April he had caught a cold, on 12 August he wrote 'labour is the curse of the world',[9] and on 22 August he wrote to Sophia 'we must not lean upon the community. Whatever is to be done, must be done by thy husband's own individual strength.'[10]

Hawthorne, like many of the others, naively believed that a few hours of work a day would suffice to run a farm; the reality of the backbreaking nature of manual labour came as a shock. He wrote to Sophia, 'a man's soul may be buried and perish under a dung-heap, or in a furrow of the field'.[11] His mother and sister Elizabeth heartily disapproved of the venture, believing that he was too good for manual labour: 'What is the use of burning your brains out in the sun, when you can do anything better with them?'[12] The communal atmosphere of the Farm was not suited to Hawthorne; as a contemporary wrote: 'He was morbidly shy and reserved, needing to be shielded from his fellows. . . . He was therefore not amenable to the democratic influences at the Community.'[13] As Hawthorne wrote to Sophia: 'the real Me was never an associate of the community'.[14]

The Blithedale Romance is Hawthorne's only full-length work employing a first-person narrator. In his diary, Hawthorne calls himself 'a mere spectator both of sport and serious business', the same posture as that of his narrator, Miles Coverdale. Hawthorne's description of how he 'lay under the trees and looked on' is akin to Coverdale's persistent voyeurism in the romance, a similarity noted by a number of critics.[15] Throughout the novel, the reader is locked into Coverdale's consciousness, and experiences all the events in the romance just as Coverdale does. But because very soon into the narrative Coverdale exposes his fantasy system as being extremely hostile towards women and persecutory of them, for the feminist reader the experience of reading *The Blithedale Romance* is terrifying because the psychopathology of the narrator's misogyny becomes the 'normal' way of viewing women within the novel.

On the eve of his departure for Blithedale, Coverdale attends 'the wonderful exhibition of the Veiled Lady', 'enshrouded within the misty drapery of a veil' insulating 'her from the material world', who is 'in the management of' (5–6) a male medium or clairvoyant. Coverdale is enthralled by the spectacle, but he does not realize that the Veiled Lady's fate is a metaphor for the condition of women in nineteenth-century American society, entrapped within a definition of femininity controlled by men, which American feminists were challenging with ever-increasing urgency and vigour. Despite his arguments to the contrary, it is a view of womankind which Coverdale himself shares.

As the teller of this tale, Miles Coverdale himself acts the male medium to Zenobia and Priscilla, to Hollingsworth and Westervelt: he is in total control of how he depicts them, and his portraits depend more upon how he perceives them, than upon how they really are. When Coverdale visits Moodie, he relates the history of how Zenobia and Priscilla are half-sisters, and that Zenobia was the daughter of Moodie's years of privilege, and Priscilla, the daughter of Moodie's years of destitution. Rather than attempt realism in the retelling, however, Coverdale says that he will 'sketch [the visit to Moodie] . . . mainly from fancy' (190). And when Coverdale comes upon Zenobia, Priscilla, and Hollingsworth in the woods, and Zenobia is visibly shaken, rather than attempting to discover what has really happened, Coverdale says 'I was left to my own conjectures' (215–16), and it is these conjectures—about how Zenobia is the victim of an unrequited love for Hollingsworth—that he reports for the reader.

Coverdale interprets virtually all of the events which he witnesses through the lenses of his own set of assumptions about the world, and most particularly, about the relationship of women and men. According to Coverdale, women are condemned to falling in love with men who will either reject them or abuse them, because men are brutes and women are victims, and he needs to see women either as saint-like, madonna-like, and passive, or as sinners and whores. He is incapable of believing that women need not fit into his category system. He paints Priscilla as the passive, wan, ethereal woman, despite evidence to the contrary; although he admits that Priscilla 'played more pranks, and perpetuated more mischief, than any other girl . . . everybody . . . considered her not quite able to look after her own interests, or fight her battle with the world' (74). And he persistently develops this view in the images he chooses to represent her: she is 'a slim and unsubstantial girl' (26), a 'flower-shrub that had done its best to blossom in too scanty light' (27), 'a leaf, floating on the dark current of events', 'a figure in a dream' (168).

Although Coverdale knows that Zenobia is both a writer and an advocate of women's rights, he sees her at first, with no evidence at all, as 'a sister of the Veiled Lady' (45). Coverdale needs to see Zenobia as a woman who is utterly controlled by a man: he is incapable of seeing her as a woman indifferent to, or more powerful than, the men within her purview. Not only is Coverdale's equation between Zenobia and the Veiled Lady inaccurate, it suggests that a strong woman like Zenobia beyond the control of a man elicits from him an unacknowledged need to control her, in the only way that he can—through his narrative, and through the medium of his metaphor.

Because the reader is locked into Coverdale's consciousness in every incident, and because the narrator does not even pretend to accuracy in retelling what he has learned, one must never assume that Coverdale's information is anything other than his interpretation of the events in the romance which springs from a deeply-felt need to see women as victims. And Coverdale never hides this from the reader (although many readers ignore what he tells them): he knows that his narration is completely unreliable. He admits that his retelling of his experience at Blithedale was 'nothing but dream-work and enchantment'; he says his tale consists of 'vagaries . . . of the spectral throng, so apt to steal out of an unquiet heart' (206).

Indeed, he is not really concerned about what these characters are really like; he prefers his creation of their lives to learning about them. For one thing, creating them requires less risk than getting to know them; as he puts it: 'It was both sad and dangerous . . . to be in too close affinity with the passions, the errors, and the misfortunes of individuals who stood within a circle of their own' (205–6). He 'covers' them and enshrouds them with his prose, creating an illusion of what they are like rather than lifting the veil to allow himself and the reader to see them as they really are. As he himself puts it: 'I can now summon her [Zenobia] up like a ghost' (15). But lest the reader be misled into thinking that this is the posture of a pathetic outsider, the effect of Coverdale's narrative is to totally control the world that he presents to the reader—it is an immensely powerful position which is presented beneath the guise of powerlessness. Indeed, the posture of powerlessness is used by Coverdale to seduce the reader into feeling sorry for him because of his weakness. Once the reader feels sorry for Coverdale, the reader will be more willing to believe anything that he says and unwilling to see him as potentially dangerous. And he uses a variation of the same strategy with Hollingsworth and Zenobia. Soon after he arrives at Blithedale, he falls ill and they nurse him. Neither of them initially can see that this seemingly frail, needy creature is capable of a diabolical, murderous antipathy towards them.

Zenobia, however, is one character who is not altogether taken in by Coverdale, and this infuriates him, although at first the only way he demonstrates his fury is by becoming increasingly virulent in his description of her. She is well aware of Coverdale's need to misrepresent the lives of the people with whom he comes into contact. She tells him that he has misinterpreted Priscilla's past by refusing to notice important details— 'the needle marks on the tip of her forefinger' (34), her pallor, which suggests she has 'been stifled with the heat of a salamander-stove' (35). Zenobia sees this as a male characteristic; she believes that 'we women judge one another by tokens that escape the obtuseness of masculine perceptions' (34). It is a stunning insight, for Zenobia understands that men like Coverdale wish to deny the reality of women's lives by imagining their lives for them. She says that Priscilla is 'neither more nor less . . . than a seamstress from the city' (33), and whereas she looks wan because she has been overworked, Coverdale will 'think her spiritual' (34).

Zenobia mocks this tendency in Coverdale by suggesting that he 'turn the affair' of Priscilla's arrival at Blithedale 'into a ballad' (33):

> It is a grand subject. . . . The storm, the startling knock at the door, the entrance of the sable knight Hollingsworth and this shadowy snow-maiden, who, precisely at the stroke of midnight, shall melt away at my feet, in a pool of ice-cold water. (33)

This is very much like how Coverdale will later describe the event. That Zenobia places Hollingsworth in the role of the sable knight probably offends Coverdale, whose own myth about Priscilla's entrance is not vastly different from the one Zenobia imagines he might make, except that in his version,

Coverdale himself becomes the sable knight, while he turns Hollingsworth into a villain:

> When a young girl comes within the sphere of such a man, she is as perilously situated as the maiden whom, in the old classical myths, the people used to expose to a dragon. If I had any duty whatever . . . it was, to endeavor to save Priscilla . . . . (71)

Thus Coverdale sees a woman as a sacrificial victim at the altar of 'passionate love' (72). And she will find it impossible to resist this destiny. This image permits Coverdale to inflate his sense of self by a rescue fantasy: 'I would really have gone far to save Priscilla' (72), but Coverdale is deluded. He does nothing to save Priscilla; rather he inflames (or creates) Priscilla's rivalry with Zenobia for Hollingsworth: he tells Priscilla, after he is sure that she loves Hollingsworth, 'it is really a blessed thing for him to have won the sympathy of such a woman as Zenobia' (126), and he tells Zenobia, after he is sure that *she* loves Hollingsworth that he 'has certainly shown great tenderness for Priscilla' (167). In fact, Hollingsworth has shown tenderness for neither.

Although Coverdale announces himself as 'a frosty bachelor' (9), which would suggest an essential asexuality, as soon as Zenobia enters, he becomes preoccupied and then obsessed with her sexuality. When she praises his poetry, and tells him that some lines have been so powerful they have 'stolen' into her memory, he smiles and blushes, 'with excess of pleasure' (14). Zenobia has no way of knowing that causing Coverdale to feel pleasure is a risky business, and that he will convert her genuine admiration for his work, given from one writer to another, into a sexual encounter. She is 'an admirable figure of a woman', 'remarkably beautiful'. He is attracted to her and has one glimpse 'of a white shoulder'. He seems to enjoy his self-titillation, for he remarks: 'It struck me as a great piece of good-fortune that there should be just that glimpse' (15).

But unable to deal with the rush of pleasant feelings, probably because they threaten his need to remain unconnected to any other human being, Coverdale immediately separates himself from Zenobia by seeing her as somehow soiled: 'some fastidious persons might pronounce them [her charms] a little deficient in softness and delicacy' (15). Yet he spends a great deal of time thinking about her and looking at her body: 'Zenobia was truly a magnificent woman'; her dress 'could not conceal . . . the queenliness of her presence' (44): she is 'womanliness incarnated' (41). But he is a generous man, and doesn't want to keep Zenobia all to himself:

> It was wronging the rest of mankind, to retain her as the spectacle of only a few. The stage would have been her proper sphere. She should have made it a point of duty, moreover, to sit endlessly to painters and sculptors. (44)

Coverdale wishes to immobilize Zenobia in 'the cold decorum of the marble' (44) so that she will no longer tempt him. But his idea that she should become an actress or an artist's model is also prompted by his thinking about her as a writer and social reformer. Keeping her as a sexual object would prevent her from being an active woman and a feminist reformer, and would keep her in her place. He can't tolerate the fact that a woman could actively pursue a role in the world, and he insists that 'her mind was full of weeds' (44).

The prospect of social reform threatens him because he believes (rightly) that Zenobia would equalize the relationship between the sexes. As he remarks, it 'is naturally among the earliest [issues] to attract her notice' (44). One of Zenobia's aims for Blithedale is that 'we will be brethren and sisters'. Fieldwork will be designated to the strongest, regardless of sex; housework, to the weakest: 'To bake, to boil, to roast, . . . to wash, and iron, and scrub, and sweep, and, . . . to repose ourselves on knitting and sewing—these . . . must be feminine occupations for the present' (16), but later, says Zenobia, 'some of us, who wear the petticoat, will go afield, and leave the weaker brethren to take our places in the kitchen' (16).[16]

This is no small issue for Coverdale. It will mean that he, the weakest of the 'weaker brethren' will surely become an inmate of the kitchen, while Zenobia, the strongest of the sisters, will take her rightful place in the fields. And since the image of himself as effeminate terrifies him, this change Zenobia proposes to make challenges him because real men don't do housework but if they are made to do so they become something other than men.

This idea is so profoundly upsetting that Coverdale instantly reminds Zenobia that God himself decreed that women do housework as punishment for enticing Adam to eat the apple: 'the kind of labor which falls to the lot of women,' he tells her, 'is just that which chiefly distinguishes artificial life—the life of degenerated mortals—from the life of Paradise' (16). Thus her suggestion that he might some day be called upon to do housework would upset the very balance of nature and the rightful and God-given function of women and men. And so, within the logic of his system of belief, he sees her as a deviant, and soon connects her deviance with her sexuality: her laugh is 'not in the least like an ordinary woman's laugh' (16); there is a 'peculiarity' about the way she comports herself. He identifies her with Eve, the seductress, the cause of all evil—there was 'something in her manner', in her 'perfectly developed figure' that conjured Eve in her 'earliest garment' (16); she is 'an enchantress', 'a witch' (45) with magic powers; she is 'Pandora, fresh from Vulcan's workshop' (24). If the enterprise at Blithedale should fail, it will be the result of Zenobia's evil nature: 'the presence of Zenobia caused our heroic enterprise to show like an illusion, a masquerade, a pastoral, a counterfeit Arcadia, in which we grown-up men and women were making a play-day' (21).

When she teases him about not being able to don the garb of Eden until after May-day, he immediately has an erotic image of Zenobia undressed:

> these last words . . . brought up a picture of that fine, perfectly developed figure, in Eve's earliest garment. I almost fancied myself actually beholding it. Her free, careless, generous modes of expression often had this effect of creating images which, though pure, are hardly felt to be quite decorous, when born of a thought that passes between man and woman. (17)

Coverdale sometimes admits that he eroticizes Zenobia's every act: 'the fault must have been entirely in my imagination' (17) but the idea disturbs him, because such thoughts are not 'quite decorous', so he quickly blames Zenobia for arousing him: one 'felt an influence breathing out of her' (17).

He becomes obsessed with images of her in the act of intercourse, which he refers to as the 'great event of a woman's existence' (46). But because that 'great event' spoils a woman, the logical corollary is that Zenobia, whose heart 'must at least have been valuable when new' (79) is now not valuable since it has been used. He creates a marriage for her, while admitting that he has no evidence for one, primarily so that he can imagine her in the throes of sexual passion. And, although he speaks metaphorically, his images are graphic: her demeanour is 'that of a woman to whom wedlock had thrown wide the gates of mystery' (47). He believes the rumours that she and Hollingsworth are lovers, primarily so that he can fantasize about their sexual activity; and, when he sees Westervelt with Zenobia for the first time, he puts Zenobia in bed with *him*: 'the idea strangely forced itself upon me, that there was a sort of familiarity between these two companions, necessarily the result of an intimate love' (102).

Nor is that enough. Not only must Zenobia be entangled with every man Coverdale sees her with, but Zenobia must have suffered:

> I imagined that Zenobia, at an earlier period of her youth, might have fallen into the misfortune above indicated. And when her passionate womanhood . . . had discovered its mistake, there had ensued the character of eccentricity and defiance, which distinguished the more public portion of her life. (103)

But these are *his fantasies*, and not accurate representations of her life. Although he thinks that it is 'the design of fate to let me into all Zenobia's secrets' (103), this idea is delusional, for all of Zenobia's secrets are, in fact, creations of his own hyperactive fantasy.

The great debate on the issue of women's rights is taken up in the novel again and again. Although Zenobia articulates the feminist position on the limitations imposed on women, as for example when she says, 'Thus far, no woman in the world has ever once spoken out her whole heart and her whole mind. The mistrust and disapproval of the vast bulk of society throttles up, as with two gigantic hands at our throats!' (120), she capitulates to Hollingsworth's misogynist view. In keeping with his attitudes about women, Coverdale believes that only sexually frustrated women become feminists: 'I could measure Zenobia's inward trouble, by the animosity with which she now took up the general quarrel of woman against man' (120). When he argues in favour of allowing a woman to have power, he argues that it would be all right if, and only if, men gave that power to women: 'I would give her all she asks, and add a great deal more, which she will not be the party to demand, but which men, if they were generous and wise, would grant of their own free motion' (121).

This is not a revolutionary attitude but a reactionary one, in keeping with Coverdale's need to control women: Coverdale locates the source of power in men; and men give that power to women if they are generous and wise. But because no man in *The Blithedale Romance* is either generous or wise, it doesn't take very long to conclude that, according to Coverdale's schema, women will have no power at all. This puts Coverdale in the position of being able to sound as if he is arguing in favour of women, while, in fact, he continues to deny her power of her own. What the women's movement wanted (and still wants) is for women themselves to have power so that they do not need to depend upon men granting it them, which history has taught us almost never happens. In this reader's judgement, Coverdale is not sympathetic to the feminist cause, and any statements that he makes that seem sympathetic are not trustworthy within the context of his contempt for any woman when she displays anything but the most dependent attitude towards men. Coverdale's overt sympathy to the women's rights movement really obscures his deep-seated revulsion for women, and his need to be in control of them.

So when Zenobia decries the limits place upon her by her sex, he tells her bluntly that a woman 'may compensate for the lack of variety' 'by constant repetition of her one event' (60), the act of intercourse. Coverdale defines woman's destiny as a constant repetition of the act of intercourse, and he fantasizes about Zenobia constantly engaging in that act. But because love, for a woman, always ends in tragedy, his fantasies of her are essentially persecutory, for he is frequently imagining Zenobia being hurt, either emotionally or physically, by the act of love. When he imagines her being loved by Hollingsworth, he thinks, 'what if, while pressing out its fragrance, he should crush the tender rosebud in his grasp!' (79); in loving Westervelt, she is 'a woman [who] wrecks herself on such a being' (103); he believes that 'man is prone to be a brute' (73). When he sees her for the last time, he believes 'Destiny . . . could do no better for Zenobia . . . than to cause the impending rock to impend a little further, and fall upon her head' (223).

An important feature of Coverdale's erotic fantasies is that he never puts himself in the fantasy, so that he has reason to feel excluded: 'A bachelor always feels himself defrauded, when he knows, or suspects, that any woman of his acquaintance has given herself away' (48). Although he says it is 'an insufferable bore, to see one man [like Hollingsworth] engrossing every thought of all the women, and leaving his friend to shiver in outer seclusion' (126), he does not respond to any gesture of friendship from anyone, including Zenobia; rather, he is suspicious of any one who is nice to him, and really prefers to be brushed off. When Priscilla peremptorily dismisses him, 'It provoked me, yet, on the whole, was the most bewitching thing that Priscilla had ever done' (126). Indeed, it might be argued that Coverdale chooses to declare Priscilla as his unrequited love-object precisely because she brushes him off, whereas Zenobia constantly engages him in debate.

At first, when Hollingsworth nurses him back to health, Coverdale believes that his 'tenderness . . . seems to me the reflection of God's own love' (43). He believes that Hollingsworth possesses a tenderness 'which few men could resist, and no woman' (28). But homoerotic love is as problematic to Coverdale as heterosexual love. When he admits his love for Hollingsworth, he soon begins to see him as 'not altogether human', as possessing a 'dreadful peculiarity' (70). Instead of seeing Hollingsworth's attempt to get him to join him in his social reform as a gesture of comradeship, Coverdale sees it as an act of betrayal. The reasons why Coverdale's love turns to loathing are hard to decipher. In one sense, he sees Hollingsworth's tenderness as feminine: 'there was something of the woman moulded into the great, stalwart frame' (42). And because Coverdale dislikes women, he dislikes the womanly in Hollingsworth and in himself. Moreover, because he believes men 'really have no tenderness', feeling tenderly about a man makes a man into a woman. Given Coverdale's attitudes towards women, this is a fate worse than death. Thus the root cause of Coverdale's rejection of Hollingsworth's particular kind of love is not homophobia; rather, it is a fundamental misogyny.[17] It is fitting that after he says goodbye to Hollingsworth for what he believes is the last time, he goes to the 'pig-stye', where the pigs are 'the very symbols of slothful ease and sensual comfort' (143): loving Hollingsworth makes him feel like a pig.

Coverdale has the psychopathology of a peeping Tom. Unable to engage in sexuality, he is constantly on the lookout for other people's sexuality, and since he believes that women like Zenobia are constantly fornicating, Coverdale is constantly looking. He peeps out of 'the peep-holes' (208) of his hermitage, and he peeps into windows. In fact, the object of the holiday that he has arranged from Blithedale is to check in to a rooming-house, spending all his time trying to look into the windows opposite. At one point, he spends fifteen delightful minutes watching a young man at his toilet.

But when Zenobia sees him peeping, and pulls down the windowshade, preventing him from indulging in that which gives him the most pleasure and power, his delusional system becomes even more pathological, overtly hostile, and, ultimately, murderous. Manifesting an attitude that many men share, he believes that looking at her is his God-given right: she is an object for him to scrutinize and she is not permitted privacy:

> I had a keen, revengeful sense of the insult inflicted by Zenobia's scornful recognition, and more particularly by her letting down the curtain; as if such were the proper barrier to be interposed between a character like hers, and a perceptive faculty like mine. (160)

His response to Zenobia's act is truly insane—he states that he has been chosen by God to watch Zenobia's behaviour and to judge it; if he decides that she should be punished, he will persecute her and he will then tell the world about it:

> True, again, I might give my full assent to the punishment which was sure to follow. But it would be given mournfully, and with undiminished love. And, after all was finished, I would come, as if to gather up the white ashes of those who had perished at the stake, and to tell the world—the wrong being now atoned for—how much had perished there. . . . (161)

It is clear from the first that Coverdale wants a tragic end to this drama. Soon after his arrival at Blithedale, his dreams include 'a dim shadow of . . . catastrophe' (38). Although he sees himself as an outside observer, and presents himself as such to the reader, the end of the novel is shrouded in mystery. In fact, Coverdale urges the tragedy along: as he himself admits 'I began to long for a catastrophe' (157).

Although most readers conclude, with the narrator, that Zenobia commits suicide because of her unrequited love for Hollingsworth, this reader is not so sure that Coverdale's version of what happens to Zenobia can be taken as accurate. Because Coverdale's delusional system insists upon Zenobia's death as a result of unrequited love, it is entirely likely that his narrative 'covers' what happens to her. All the reader knows for certain is that Zenobia's body is found in a river. No one but Coverdale supplies the interpretation of Zenobia's death as suicide.

Indeed, within the context of the novel, that Zenobia was murdered is as likely a conclusion as that she committed suicide, and given the content of Coverdale's consciousness, he would be a likely suspect.[18] A careful reading of chapter XXVI, 'Zenobia and Coverdale', is illuminating in this regard. Because he believes that Zenobia loves Hollingsworth, he feels excluded: he states that Zenobia 'had entirely forgotten me' (222). When he hears her crying, although he states that he wishes to comfort her, his fantasy indicates that he wants to hurt her. He believes that the only cure for Zenobia's grief is death—'Destiny ... could do no better for Zenobia, in the way of quick relief, than to cause the impending rock to impend a little further, and fall upon her head' (223). But when she tells him that 'Lip of man will never touch my hand again. I intend to become a Catholic, for the sake of going into a nunnery' (227), she refuses to play the part that he has outlined for her. Earlier in the novel, Coverdale demonstrated that he needed to see Zenobia as a sexual object, and that an important part of his delusional system was that her body be available to him for fantasy. When she tells him she is not going to kill herself for love, but instead, that she will withdraw to a nunnery, she defies his system in several ways. First, if we take her at her word, in a nunnery she will be asexual, married to God, committed to a life of sexual abstinence. Second, 'behind the black-veil' (228), no man, certainly not Coverdale, will be allowed to look at her. It is entirely possible that this statement elicits similar feelings—ones of murderous rage—in Coverdale as did Zenobia's earlier act of drawing the curtain. For Zenobia's donning the veil will prevent Coverdale from ever seeing her again, and because he believes it is his God-given right to see her, is it also not entirely possible that he should intervene to prevent her from pulling the curtain down for ever?

Indeed, if anyone but Coverdale were reporting the events of Zenobia's death, he would immediately be suspected of murder, even if in fact he did not murder her. According to his testimony, although she leaves him, he 'was affected with a fantasy that Zenobia had not actually gone, but was still hovering about the spot, and haunting it'. He describes her character as 'a brilliant stain upon the air'. He 'must have fallen asleep, and had a dream, all the circumstances of which utterly vanished at the moment when they converged to some tragical catastrophe' (228). Throughout the novel, Coverdale has thought about the death of each of the characters, and, more than once, he has thought of himself as an agent of death, particularly in the scene following Zenobia's pulling the shade down. He wonders 'who, of all these strong men, and fair women and maidens, is doomed the first to die' (130). He sees himself as an agent of God's will: he believes that he has the right to ascertain who is good and who is evil.

Coverdale is the last person who sees Zenobia alive. Although she does not mention suicide to him, but rather tells him 'I intend to become a Catholic, for the sake of going into a nunnery' (227), he tells Hollingsworth he believes she drowned herself, even before anyone knows she's missing. He has her handkerchief, and although he shows it to Silas Forster and Hollingsworth no one questions how he has come by it; his own version of his last moments with her makes no mention of a handkerchief. He leads them to 'the particular spot, on the river-bank, which I had paused to contemplate, in the course of my afternoon's ramble', where they find Zenobia's shoe. The narrator does not tell us, and no reader has questioned, how he knows the precise spot where she has entered the river. Coverdale tells the reader it was a 'nameless presentiment' (231).

In fact, Westervelt seriously challenges Coverdale's version of the events which have transpired, but because Coverdale discredits Westervelt as a character, his suspicions about Coverdale's version are glossed by the reader. When Coverdale states that Zenobia committed suicide because of love, Westervelt counters with the fact that it was entirely outside of Zenobia's character to end her life for love: 'Love had failed her. ... Had it never failed her before? Yet she survived it' (240). Coverdale insists that Zenobia is better off dead: 'I cannot deem it a misfortune that she sleeps in yonder grave' (240), which exposes his underlying desire to annihilate her, and when Westervelt challenges him again, saying that he cannot believe she has thrown away 'Twenty years of a brilliant lifetime ... for a mere woman's whim', Coverdale thinks, 'Heaven deal with Westervelt according to his nature and deserts!—that is to say, annihilate him' (240). Any man who prefers a woman like Zenobia alive should, like Zenobia, die.

Virtually all of the criticism that focuses upon the fact that Coverdale's narrative cannot be trusted takes the view that Coverdale is a weak character. James H. Justus's view, in 'Hawthorne's Coverdale', is illustrative; for Justus, Coverdale is 'a failed human being' (23), a man who 'dooms himself irrevocably to a life of sterile complacency' (26) because of his 'emotional deficiency' (31). Alfred Rosa sees 'parallels between Coverdale's situation and Hawthorne's' (135); he argues that 'Coverdale is sexually frustrated' (141), that he is 'parasitic' (142), but he acknowledges that his 'occasional probes into the private lives of his friends may have speeded their tragedies' (142).

James R. Mellow in *Nathaniel Hawthorne in His Times* has written that *The Blithedale Romance* is so sympathetic to the issue of women's rights that 'it could easily have been written by one of the professed champions of women's rights' (396). For Mellow, and for others, like Nina Baym, who read the novel in this way, Hawthorne uses Zenobia as a mouthpiece to put forth his own ideas about the limitations of the male sex: as Zenobia phrases it, 'In denying us our rights, he betrays even more blindness to his own interests' (395–6); indeed, Mellow believes it is 'a book about sexual politics' (396). Herbert Hoeltje too has stated in *Inward Sky* that the novel expresses 'a protest against both the nineteenth-century status of woman' (388), and 'the masculine egotism which tended to make woman a gentle parasite' (390). Hoeltje has observed that 'when

Hawthorne wrote [the novel], Margaret Fuller had recently drowned in a shipwreck off Fire Island' (384), and he believes that Fuller was very much in Hawthorne's mind when he constructed his character Zenobia.[19]

Rudolph Von Abele, in *The Death of the Artist*, maintains, however, that Zenobia is 'never really permitted to think' (79) and that her 'feminism, indeed, rests on her sexuality' (79). Rather than seeing the novel as sympathetic to feminism, Von Abele argues that Hawthorne criticizes the feminist position by having Zenobia's feminism collapse the moment that Hollingsworth challenges it. Zenobia, moreover, responds, not like a feminist, but like 'any proper nineteenth-century woman, by directing her resentment and frustration . . . at herself' (79). He points out that the name Zenobia means 'having life from Zeus' (80), which is the quintessential misogynist position, that feminine life depends upon the male. Morton Cronin's indictment of Hawthorne's attitude towards women's rights in 'Hawthorne on romantic love and the status of women' is even more severe: he believes that, confronted 'with the issue of women's rights, this gifted analyst . . . utters the stalest of all judgments. . . . But Hawthorne is not content simply to utter the sentiment. He forces his heroine to prove the truth of it in her relations with Hollingsworth' (92).

Allan and Barbara Lefcowitz in 'Some rents in the veil' have pointed out that much of the ambiguity of the novel has to do with 'the propriety of certain intense but dangerous psychosexual feelings, as reflected in the double-edged portraits of Priscilla and Zenobia' (264). Rather than seeing Priscilla as emblematic of *naïveté*, the authors argue that 'at least part of Priscilla's strangely cloistered past was spent in the practice of sexual activities of less than a pristine or conventionally wholesome nature' (267), that she was, in all likelihood, a prostitute. The authors argue that Coverdale chooses Priscilla as a love object, 'not because she is better than Zenobia, but because he too is afraid of Zenobia's power' (275).

The feminist historian Annette Kolodny, in her Introduction to *The Blithedale Romance* states that Hawthorne wrote the novel during a time when the United States was facing severe economic problems as a result of the financial panic of 1837, which had resulted in 'an underclass of urban poor' (xi). In response to 'urban poverty, increased crime, and general moral decay', 'philanthropic organizations sprang up to attempt the rehabilitation of criminals, the protection of prostitutes, and the care of orphans and paupers' (xii). Brook Farm was one of the many 'idealistic blueprints for social and economic harmony' (xii). According to Kolodny, it was the turmoil of the period which 'helped to create recognizable characters in a philanthropist like Hollingsworth, an intellectual feminist like Zenobia, and a poor, exploited seamstress like Priscilla' (xii). The novel became a tale of 'failed possibilities and multiple human betrayals' (xviii), of 'the pervasive failure of "love and free-heartedness" between and among them' (xx). The 'disjunction between what the Blithedalers espouse and what they actually experience gives *The Blithedale Romance* its peculiar fascination' (xx).

Kolodny emphasizes that readers should not trust Miles Coverdale's version of the events: 'they find themselves at odds with the conclusions that Coverdale is drawing from his limited observations and seemingly unlimited fantasies' (xxiii); rather, he 'has constructed his narrative so as to confirm his present fixed belief that any vision "worth the having . . . is certain never to be consummated otherwise than by a failure"' (xxvi). She interprets Coverdale as a man who is 'no idealist'; instead, he is 'a consummate creator of imagined fictions' (xxvii), and the only thing that he is capable of accomplishing in life is his narrative, 'a chronicle of failure and betrayal, emanating from a man whose "own life [is] all an emptiness"' (xxx).

Wendy Martin, in 'Seduced and abandoned in the New World' reads the novel as a 'secular version of *The Scarlet Letter*' (230) in which Coverdale's preference for the 'gentle parasite' Priscilla perhaps echoed 'Hawthorne himself, who had strong antifeminist predilections' (230). Thus, Zenobia's capitulation to Hollingsworth's egotism and his definition of woman '"as man's subordinate"' can be read as

Hawthorne's attempt to undermine the feminist movement's search for greater equality. Sandra Gilbert and Susan Gubar in *Madwoman in the Attic* suggest that the image of 'the veiled woman reflects male dread of women' (472), but they also underscore that the 'veiled lady becomes a strategy for survival in a hostile, male-dominated world' (473).

The feminist Nina Baym in 'The significance of plot in Hawthorne's romances' reads *The Blithedale Romance* as a novel which exposes the ostensible beliefs of each of the central characters as shams: 'Hollingsworth is no philanthropist, Zenobia no feminist, and Blithedale Farm is not a socialist community' (63): 'Zenobia's behaviour toward Priscilla shows no feelings of sisterhood, while her behaviour toward Hollingsworth' indicates that she wishes to 'be owned by a powerful, patriarchal male' (63). Thus, she is 'only a pretender to feminism' (64).

In *The Shape of Hawthorne's Career*, Baym reads Coverdale's passivity as an index of 'his oppression and inhibition' (187). She believes that the expression of his 'violent antagonism represents the fragmentation of a personality' (187). Baym argues that one of the major points of the novel is 'the idea that a man's liberation and fulfillment require his accepting a more fully sexual image of woman than the culture allows' (191); Coverdale's creative energies 'are blocked because he cannot accept the passionate foundation of the human character and the inextricable union of art and Eros' (192). Just as Zenobia represents 'the natural or precivilized woman, or the future possibility of woman, Priscilla is the woman in history'—she 'represents the whole range of exploited female roles in society'; her 'economic servitude is recapitulated on a psychosexual level in the murky symbol of the Veiled Lady' (196). Although she is seen as 'a spiritual being', this obscures the fact that 'she is really a possessed creature, owned and exploited' (197). Baym suggests that Hawthorne is criticizing a society in which 'young, frail, immature girls become objects of sexual interest while fully sexed adult women are experienced as frightening, corrupt, or repellent' (197).

By the end of the novel, whether or not Coverdale's perceptions of the events surrounding Zenobia's death are in fact true, they become true for the reader, which is one of the most problematic issues in the novel for the feminist reader. A reader can never know whether or not Coverdale did, in fact, kill Zenobia. But by the time that Coverdale reports Zenobia's death as suicide, the reader's perception of the event becomes so beclouded by Coverdale's power as a narrator, that most readers believe him, and never pause to question whether or not he is reliable. Indeed, no one but Westervelt counters Coverdale's story because Coverdale's story reproduces what the society wants to believe and needs to believe about what happened to Zenobia—she becomes a 'typical' woman by her suicide, and this absolves them from having to deal with the possibility that she was the victim of foul play.

The reader, thus, chooses to ignore that Coverdale wanted to kill her, that he has her handkerchief, and that he knows precisely where she died. In any mystery novel, these events would be seized upon by even the most casual reader, but they are ignored in *The Blithedale Romance*. Thus, the reader becomes co-conspirator with Coverdale as Coverdale kills Zenobia into art. By the end of the novel, Coverdale has punished Zenobia by creating a 'ballad' with her as subject in which she, a well-known writer, social reformer, and feminist, plays the most overworked, clichéd, and stereotyped role a woman can have—a woman who drowns herself for the unrequited love of a man who is himself a misogynist. Although the reader surely cannot trust what Coverdale has said about Zenobia, the force of his fantasy system is so overwhelming, so powerful, and so consistent with prevailing views about feminine behaviour, that his perverted version of the story becomes the only truth the reader can see. Indeed, Coverdale is no more, no less psychopathic in his treatment of Zenobia and in his attitudes and actions towards her than any misogynist would be, but that fact is elided in the text, and the psychopathology of Coverdale's misogyny begins to seem normal, because of the way the novel is told. Most readers forget, or prefer to ignore, that we take as true a version of the events provided by a narrator who hated her sex and who wanted her dead. Because so much of woman's history is told by a narrator who shares Coverdale's point of view, we accept Coverdale's story as true, and his point of view as normal. It may be normal, but it is, at the same time, an extreme form of pathology. The most upsetting moment in the romance is Zenobia's death viewed as an event to be applauded within the context of a view of the world that wants her dead, and the subsequent loss of Zenobia's story. For the reader will never know what happened to Zenobia, and the supplanting of her story with a psychopathic murderous misogynist's version of her story is, for this reader, the real text of *The Blithedale Romance*.

Epilogue

The ending of each of the novels discussed in this work presents the reader with a graphic and unrelenting view of the tragic results of feminine powerlessness. By the end of *Fanshawe*, Butler's mother has died in abject poverty, with no way to sustain life, having been abandoned by her son, her only source of income; Ellen Langton has married Walcott, a potential wife-beater, the inevitable outcome of a family history of her father's abandonment and lack of care, her only way of controlling Walcott's violence being to adopt an attitude of demure helplessness. By the end of *The Scarlet Letter*, the reader knows that Mistress Hibbins, who needs her brother's protection for she has no way to sustain herself, will in all likelihood be prosecuted as a witch because she has become a nuisance to her brother and an embarrassment to him; Hester Prynne is living out her life on the fringes of society, striving to support herself by her needlework, having been abandoned by her daughter Pearl, whose primary allegiance in her adult years is not to the mother who cared for her, fought to keep her, and nourished her through the most desperate times, but, instead, to the husband who married her and who sends her mother trinkets rather than sustenance. *The House of the Seven Gables* ends with Hepzibah imprisoned within her position as a lady, with Phoebe married to a man who wants to control her, and who has written a tale in which a woman dies at the hands of a male who controls her. And by the end of *The Blithedale Romance*, Priscilla is married to Hollingsworth, an avowed misogynist and probable homosexual, who has, in all likelihood, married her for her money; while Zenobia's mysterious death is commonly held to have been a love death.

If this corpus had been written by a woman, the critic might argue that the writer was preoccupied with the unremittingly disastrous consequences to women of a society which refused to allow them equality under the law, of a society which insisted, in fact, that they be treated as the property of men. But because Hawthorne has chosen the form of the romance,[1] which blunts the realism of the events, and obscures the moral or ethical conclusions which might be drawn from such portraits, at the end of each of the novels, the destitute circumstances of the women portrayed get lost in a language which either obfuscates or deliberately distorts what has happened to them.

Thus, by the end of each of the novels, the reader is trapped within a misogynist point of view which makes it difficult, if not impossible, to see clearly what has really happened to each of the women in the novel. The most extreme example of this is, of course, the end of *The Blithedale Romance*, in which the reader is trapped within the consciousness of a murderous maniac, but is so seduced by his power to control the narrative that the reader never acknowledges the possibility that this man is deadly. The end of *Blithedale* is essentially no different from the end of *Fanshawe*, with Walcott in control; than the end of *The Scarlet Letter*, with the narrator of 'The Custom-House' in control of a narrative which has adulterated the facts of women's history during the Puritan era; which is, in turn, no different from the end of *House of the Seven Gables*, with both women submerged by the reigning forces of the patriarchy.

Hawthorne has provided a galaxy of terrifying men who present themselves to the world and to the women in their lives as helpless, hapless, and pathetic. The narrators of each of the Prefaces, Butler, Walcott, Chillingworth, the brother of Mistress Hibbins, the Puritan oligarchs,

Holgrave, Judge Pyncheon, Clifford Pyncheon, Coverdale, and Hollingsworth, abandon the women in their lives, allow them to die in poverty, abduct them, threaten them, incarcerate them, indict them, sentence them to death, tell stories in which they die, revise their stories so that what happened to them will not appear so odious, have fantasies about murdering them and visions of rocks falling on their heads, celebrate their death rather than their lives, blame them for all the evil in the world, burn them as witches, take their property, deny them an income, try to take their children, imprison them within the role of lady, of prostitute, of veiled lady, of madonna, force them to live on the fringes of society.

In fact, they are, within their hearts, all potentially vicious and violent: some, like the Puritan oligarchs, and perhaps even Coverdale, in fact kill women, often with society's sanction and praise; and if they do not, in fact, act on their unconscious or conscious murderous feelings towards women, it is only by chance, not because their society disallows this behaviour. In fact, what is so terrifying about Hawthorne's works is that his women have no legal recourse, no societal sanction against these men. Rather, these men, perverse as they are, are precisely what the patriarchy produces to represent true manhood, and, like the Puritan hierarchy, in some instances they become the heroes of their times.

Hawthorne's greatest success as a novelist is that he portrayed, with superb accuracy, the condition of women in the nineteenth century and the psychological processes of men who could not tolerate the notion of female equality. But, after being apprised, in novel after novel, by narrator after narrator, that no reform, no change in the condition of women is possible because social structures are rooted in what might as well be human nature, reading Hawthorne, for the women reader, is ultimately a disheartening, if not somewhat persecutory experience. For a feminist, his greatest failure as a writer was that, because he shared the misogynist view of his age, he could not condemn what he saw and drew back from defining the implications, for society, of what he so astutely observed about the reality of women's lives.

As a woman, this reader would prefer to live anywhere rather than in the universe of Hawthorne's fiction, but the universe of Hawthorne's fiction is an accurate representation of a patriarchy gone mad with misogyny, and depicts quite accurately the world in which virtually all women live.

Notes

In these notes, the reader will find the titles of all works quoted: the subtitles, and all publishing information are to be found in the Select Bibliography.

Preface

1. L. A. DeSalvo, 'Literature and sexuality', p. 33. *See also*, J. McWalters, 'In defense of poor Hester', and L. A. DeSalvo, '"An earthly story with a hellish meaning"', pp. 36–7.
2. D. H. Lawrence, *Studies in Classic American Literature*, p. 92.
3. J. R. Mellow, *Nathaniel Hawthorne in His Times*, pp. 25–34.
4. J. W. Bicknell, '*The Marble Faun* reconsidered', p. 193.
   This study also does not take up those works which Hawthorne did not complete in his lifetime (*The Ancestral Footstep*, *Dr. Grimshawe's Secret*, *Septimus Felton*, and *The Dolliver Romance*), his historical tales for children, or his short tales, or *The Marble Faun*, set in Rome, although there is much in these works that is of interest to feminists. Unless otherwise indicated, the quotations from Hawthorne's works are taken from *The Centenary Edition of The Works of Nathaniel Hawthorne* published by the Ohio State University Press. The complete citation for each volume is listed in the Bibliography; each chapter contains, within parentheses, the page number where that quotation can be found.
5. C. M. Simpson, Introduction to *The Centenary Edition of The Works of Nathaniel Hawthorne*, *The Marble Faun: or, The Romance of Monte Beni*, pp. xxxvii, xxxviii.

Chapter One Nathaniel Hawthorne and Feminists

1. K. Millett, *Sexual Politics*, p. 66. *See* M. Vicinus, ed., *A Widening Sphere*; A. Douglas, *The Feminization of American Culture*;

B. Epstein, 'Family, sexual morality, and popular movements in turn-of-the-century America' in A. Snitow, *et al.*, eds, *Powers of Desire*; M. Fuller, *Woman in the Nineteenth Century*; E. Flexner, *Century of Struggle*; M. P. Ryan, *Womanhood in America*; C. Smith-Rosenberg, 'The female world of love and ritual'. J. Fryer, *The Faces of Eve*.

2. On Martineau and Jewsbury, *see* J. R. Mellow, *Nathaniel Hawthorne in His Times*, pp. 441, 174; on Fuller, *see* J. Hawthorne, *Nathaniel Hawthorne and His Wife*, I, pp. 256 ff.; on the Peabody sisters, *see* L. H. Tharp, *The Peabody Sisters of Salem*.
3. J. R. Mellow, p. 14. *See* E. Ross and R. Rapp, 'Sex and society', in A. Snitow, *et al.*, eds, *Powers of Desire*; V. Loggins, *The Hawthornes*, p. 206.
4. V. Loggins, p. 209.
5. *See* B. Epstein; *and also* G. C. Erlich, *Family Themes and Hawthorne's Fiction*. For his description of these times as a long 'Lent', *see* N. Hawthorne, *Love Letters*, II, p. 114.
6. M. D. Bell, *Hawthorne and the Historical Romance of New England*, p. vii.
7. C. Berryman, *From Wilderness to Wasteland*, p. 130; *sce also* V. Loggins.
8. C. Berryman, pp. 128, 129. For critical works exploring the relationship between Hawthorne and his ancestors, see, especially, M. D. Bell, C. Berryman, and V. Loggins. Berryman (p. 127) describes Hawthorne's familiarity with works such as Cotton Mather's *Christi Americana* and Felt's *Annals of Salem*.
9. M. D. Bell, p. 34.
10. *See* M. Daly, *Beyond God the Father* and A. Dworkin, *Woman Hating*.
11. N. F. Doubleday, 'Hawthorne's Hester and feminism', p. 828.
12. N. F. Doubleday, p. 826.
13. J. Hawthorne describes Hawthorne's meeting in 1856 with Coventry Patmore, and his 'Angel in the House' as 'a poem which Hawthorne had been greatly pleased with, as he now was with its author' (p. 151). *See also* C. Christ, 'Victorian masculinity and the angel in the house', in M. Vicinus, ed., pp. 146–62.
14. N. F. Doubleday, p. 827. *See* M. J. Colacurcio, 'Footsteps of Ann Hutchinson'; D. Leverenz, 'Mrs. Hawthorne's headache'; M. Cronin, 'Hawthorne on romantic love and the status of women'; F. I. Carpenter, 'Scarlet A minus'; and J. Fryer, *The Faces of Eve*. pp. 76–7.
15. N. F. Doubleday, p. 827, quoting Hawthorne.
16. The sketch can be found in *The Complete Writings of Nathaniel Hawthorne*, vol. XVII, *Miscellanies*. Reference to page numbers within the text are to this edition. *See* M. D. Bell, p. 46.
17. Hawthorne to his publisher J. T. Ticknor, quoted in J. W. Warren, *The American Narcissus*, p. 191.

18. Emphasis added.
19. According to V. Loggins, p. 33, William Hathorne, because he was no longer a member of the General Court which tried her, 'had no direct part in the trial', but he no doubt 'thanked God when his enemies triumphed and sentenced her to banishment'. In this regard, it is important to note that Sophia Peabody wrote to her mother on 17 November 1847 that she and Nathaniel 'went to . . . see an old book once belonging to our distinguished ancestor William Hathorne, 1634' (J. Hawthorne, p. 311).
20. *See especially* M. D. Bell, p. 100 ff.
21. B. Welter, *Dimity Convictions*, 94. In *The Scarlet Letter*, Hester ponders 'the coming of a female saviour. She reflects that because of her sin she is no longer worthy to be chosen' (B. Welter, p. 87).
22. B. Welter, p. 94.
23. *See* A. Douglas, 'Margaret Fuller and the disavowal of fiction', *The Feminization of American Culture*, pp. 259–87; B. G. Chevigny, 'The long arm of censorship'; J. W. Warren, pp. 210–11.
24. B. Welter, p. 14.
25. J. Hawthorne, I, p. 257.
26. J. Hawthorne, I, p. 261.
27. B. Welter, p. 4.
28. B. Welter, pp. 71, 77, 76.
29. J. W. Warren, p. 8.
30. N. Baym, *Women's Fiction*, p. 12.
31. N. Baym, *Women's Fiction*, p. 18.
32. *See* M. Kelley, *Private Woman, Public Stage*.
33. J. W. Warren, p. 261.
34. J. W. Warren, p. 191, quoting Hawthorne.
35. L. H. Tharp, pp. 33, 39.
36. J. Hawthorne, I, p. 45.
37. R. M. Baylor, *Elizabeth Palmer Peabody*, p. 164.
38. L. H. Tharp, p. 87.
39. For a complete listing of her writings, *see* R. M. Baylor.
40. L. H. Tharp, pp. 88, 90, 94, 103, 106, 138, 142, 324.
41. J. W. Warren, pp. 298–9.
42. L. H. Tharp, pp. 126, 117.
43. E. P. Peabody to H. Mann, 3 March 1838, Horace Mann Collection, Massachusetts Historical Society, quoted in R. M. Baylor, p. 75. Peabody's reviews of Hawthorne's works are 'The genius of N. Hawthorne', *Atlantic Monthly*, XXII, September 1868; 'Hawthorne. *The Blithedale Romance*', *North American Review*, LXXVI, 1853; 'Hawthorne's *The Marble Faun*', *Atlantic Monthly*, XXII, September 1868.
44. N. Hawthorne, *Love Letters*, 27 June 1848, II, p. 184.
45. L. H. Tharp, p. 190.
46. J. W. Warren, p. 204.
47. J. Hawthorne, I, pp. 39, 199, 254.

48. T. W. Herbert, 'Numinous mates', p. 4.
49. J. W. Warren, pp. 207–8.
50. T. W. Herbert, p. 20.
51. J. W. Warren, p. 204, quoting N. Hawthorne, *Love Letters*, I, p. 202.
52. J. W. Warren, p. 204, quoting N. Hawthorne, *Love Letters*, I, p. 202.
53. N. Hawthorne, *Love Letters*, I, p. 25.
54. *See especially* 3 October 1839, N. Hawthorne, *Love Letters*, I, 68–9; J. Hawthorne, p. 103.
55. N. Hawthorne, *Love Letters*, I, p. 43; II, p. 26.
56. J.Hawthorne, pp. 273, 277, 313.
57. Sophia Peabody wrote: 'Home, I think is the greatest arena for women, and there, I am sure, she can wield a power which no king or conqueror can cope with' (J. W. Warren, p. 203, quoting Sophia as quoted in J. Hawthorne, I, pp. 256–7).
58. N. Hawthorne, *Twenty Days with Julian and Little Bunny*, p. 8.
59. J. Hawthorne, II, p. 267.
60. L. H. Tharp, pp. 229, 308, 161.
61. L. H. Tharp, p. 287. According to his son, Julian, Hawthorne 'regarded slavery as an evil, and would have made any personal sacrifice to be rid of it, as an element in the national existence; but to maintain that we were ready to imperil our life merely out of regard for the liberation of the negroes was, in his opinion, to utter sentimental nonsense' (p. 271).
62. L. H. Tharp, p. 288. Hawthorne had written the official biography of his friend Franklin Pierce when he ran for President, and, according to Horace Mann, Pierce would be the 'merest tool of slavery' (L. H. Tharp, p. 273). Mann's prediction was correct, for during the Pierce administration 'anti-slavery had lost ground' (L. H. Tharp, p. 273). H. Mann, regarding Hawthorne's biography of Pierce, wrote: 'If he makes out Pierce to be a great man or a brave man, it will be the greatest work of fiction he ever wrote' (L. H. Tharp, p. 221).

    Elizabeth, at age eighty-three, writing to Horatio Bridge, said that Hawthorne 'knew *nothing* about slavery—he had never been at the South. He never saw a slave or a fugitive slave. He looked at all anti-slavery literature as beneath the consideration of a reasonable man' (J. R. Mellow, p. 568). See, however, Hawthorne's entry for 11 August 1838 in *The American Notebooks*:

    > I saw one old negro, a genuine specimen of the slave-negro, without any of the foppery of the race of our parts; and old fellow with a bag, I suppose of broken victuals on his shoulders; . . . full of grimaces, and ridiculous antics, laughing laughably, yet without affectation—then talking with a strange kind of pathos, about

> the whippings he used to get, while he was a slave—a queer thing of mere feeling, with some glimmerings of sense.(112)

He also describes another 'gray old negro, but of a different stamp, politic, sage . . . talking about the rights of his race. . . .' Hawthorne concludes: 'On the whole, I find myself rather more of an abolitionist in feeling than in principle' (p. 112). An entry for 9 September 1838 describes a 'negro respectably dressed'; Hawthorne concludes: 'the negro was really so human—and to talk of owning a thousand like him . . .' (p. 151).

63. T. W. Herbert, 'Little Pearl and Hawthorne's daughter', pp. 29, 12, 21.
64. T. W. Herbert, pp. 1, 33.
65. T. W. Herbert, p. 33.
66. L. H. Tharp, p. 303.

Chapter Two Feminists and Nathaniel Hawthorne

1. *See* A. Kolodny, *The Lay of the Land* for a complete exploration of this idea.
2. L. Fiedler's argument in *Love and Death in the American Novel* is similar: 'the novel was a kind of conduct book for the daughters of the bourgeoisie, aimed at teaching obedience to parents and wariness before potential seducers' with 'vice punished and virtue rewarded' (45).
3. L. Fiedler's thesis is that the need to punish women in American literature has its roots in a Puritan bias, rooted in a theology which sees women as responsible for Adam's expulsion from the garden of Eden, coupled with a male terror of sexuality. Thus women are depicted as either saints or sinners, as either goddesses or whores, and the fictional vision is always bifurcated and never represents women characters as fully realized, and fully human.
4. W. H. Shurr describes an important moment in Hawthorne's *Mosses from an Old Manse* in which he ponders 'questions raised by New England transcendentalism in relation to sexual fulfillment and the myth of the lost Garden Paradise' (144). Shurr argues that each of Hawthorne's novels, and many of the tales, including 'The New Adam and Eve' and 'Rappaccini's Daughter' are a comment upon and reinterpretation of the Garden of Eden myth.
5. N. Baym's feminist scholarship is extremely important and will be referred to throughout.
6. P. Young's *Hawthorne's Secret* argues that Hawthorne's possible incestuous experience with his sister Elizabeth (Ebe) was at the core of his novelistic imagination, and that the effect of this life experience

was compounded by the story of the Manning incest trial, with which Hawthorne was surely familiar. I suspect that Hawthorne was, in fact, preoccupied with the issue of incest; it is relevant in this regard that Erlich describes Hawthorne's outburst at having to share a bed with his uncle. Hawthorne's feelings for his daughter Una were, as T. Walter Herbert has described, immensely complicated. His persecutory feelings for Una are best traced in his *The American Notebooks*. On 30 July 1849 he describes Una as 'a spirit strangely mingled with good and evil, haunting the house where I dwell' (430–1). There is one important entry in which he describes his daughter's behaviour in curious terms, considering his preoccupation with the issue of incest: 'At about six o'clock, I went to take a walk, leaving Una preparing for bed, and running about the room in her chemise, which does not come down far enough to serve the purpose of a fig-leaf; never were seen such contortions and attitudinizing—prostrating herself on all fours, and thrusting up her little bum as a spectacle to men and angels, being among the least grotesque' (417).

7. C. N. Davidson, 'The marketing of taste', p. 152.

Chapter Three Fanshawe, A Tale (1828)

1. *See* J. R. Mellow, *Nathaniel Hawthorne in His Times*, p. 33; R. H. Pearce, Introduction to *Fanshawe, The Centenary Edition of The Works of Nathaniel Hawthorne*, vol. III, p. 303. Page number references in the text are to this edition.
2. R. Stewart, *Nathaniel Hawthorne*, pp. 23–4. Elizabeth Hawthorne 'remembered a letter from Bowdoin in which he spoke of "progress on a novel"'.
3. M. D. Bell, *The Development of American Romance*, p. 128.
4. N. Baym, 'Hawthorne's gothic discards', p. 105.
5. R. Cantwell, *Nathaniel Hawthorne*, p. 119.
6. W. Martin, 'Seduced and abandoned in the New World', p. 24. R. H. Pearce, p. 312. *See* R. H. Pearce, pp. 302, 311–12. *See* J. D. Crowley, ed., *Hawthorne*, p. 9. R. Cantwell, *Nathaniel Hawthorne*, p. 122, suggests that the work was suppressed because the heroine was a fictionalized portrait of Franklin Pierce's fiancée. R. H. Pearce has suggested that Hawthorne did not want the novel identified with his name because it was a deliberately derivative novel, written in the hopes of a commercial success. Perhaps he omitted his name from the title page in deference to his fellow classmates, like Jonathan Cilley and Franklin Pierce, who were involved in politics. At about the same time that the book was published, Cilley was involved in a bitter campaign for a congressional seat in Maine, and his political chances

might have been severely damaged if his behaviour as an undergraduate was linked by his enemies to a scene like the one in which Walcott drinks himself into an abusive alcoholic frenzy.

7. J. L. Herman, with L. Hirschman, *Father-Daughter Incest*, p. 1 and following.
8. *See* C. Davidson 'Mothers and Daughters in the Fiction of the New Republic'; N. Baym, *Women's Fiction*; M. Kelley, *Private Woman, Public Stage*, and M. D. Bell, *The Development of American Romance*.
9. *See* J. Herman, p. 96 and following.
10. For an analysis of this theme, see N. Arvin, Introduction to *Hawthorne's Short Stories*, J. Fetterley, *The Resisting Reader*, L. Fiedler, *Love and Death in the American Novel*, and F. Crews, *The Sins of the Fathers*, among others.
11. *See* J. Fryer, *The Faces of Eve*.
12. J. Fetterley, p. 7.
13. R. Cantwell, p. 62. For an analysis of how Hawthorne's relationship with his mother contributed to the development of *The Scarlet Letter*, see N. Baym, 'Nathaniel Hawthorne and his mother' and G. C. Erlich, *Family Themes and Hawthorne's Fiction*.
14. *See* J. D. Crowley, ed., pp. 41–6, which reprints contemporary reviews. Page numbers in the text, referring to contemporary reviews, refer to Crowley's edition.
15. There is a similarity between Samuel Johnson's *Rasselas*, and *Fanshawe*, which has never been fully explored. Of especial interest are the gender-determined assumptions about the educational process of women and men as described in both works.

    In *House of the Seven Gables*, in Chapter IX, 'Clifford and Phoebe', Hepzibah, in an attempt to make Clifford happy, 'then took up Rasselas, and began to read of the Happy Valley, with a vague idea that some secret of a contented life had there been elaborated, which might at least serve Clifford and herself for this one day' (134). It would be worthwhile to fully explore Hawthorne's use of Johnson's work.
16. N. F. Doubleday, *Hawthorne's Early Tales*.
17. B. Welter in *Dimity Convictions* has described Ellen Langton's function as connecting the male students to earthly pursuits.

Chapter Four The Scarlet Letter, A Romance (1850)

1. N. Hawthorne, *The American Notebooks*, p. 254.
2. N. Arvin, Introduction to *Hawthorne's Short Stories*, p. 254.
3. For a history of the publication of these volumes, see F. Bowers

'Textual commentary' in N. Hawthorne, *Twice-Told Tales, The Centenary Edition of the Works of Nathaniel Hawthorne*, vol. IX, and J. D. Crowley's 'Historical commentary' in *Mosses from an Old Manse, The Centenary Edition of the Works of Nathaniel Hawthorne*, vol. X. The final collection to appear in Hawthorne's lifetime was *The Snow-Image* (1851). *See* J. D. Crowley, 'Historical commentary' in *The Snow-Image and Uncollected Tales, The Centenary Edition of the Works of Nathaniel Hawthorne*, vol. XI.

Virtually all of Hawthorne's short fiction is of interest to the feminist reader, and a complete study of his short works from a feminist perspective is sorely needed, but could not be included in this volume because of space limitations. A considerable number of the stories deal with the issue of love and marriage, such as 'The Wedding Knell', 'The Minister's Black Veil', 'The Birth-mark', 'The New Adam and Eve', to name but a few, and they offer superb insights, not only into Hawthorne's attitudes, but also to the prevailing attitudes of the time. Others, such as 'Rappaccini's Daughter' and 'The Snow-Image' deal with the issue of the condition of daughterhood within the patriarchal family as Hawthorne conceived it, which illuminates his treatment of Una. Still others, like 'The Gentle Boy' and 'My Kinsman, Major Molineaux' express Hawthorne's often ambivalent attitudes to his patriarchal forebears. Certain tales, such as 'Alice Doane's Appeal' treat the issue of incest. A sketch which castigates a woman for modesty, and which illustrates Hawthorne's vacillating attitude to women's sexuality, in addition to demonstrating his voyeurism, is 'The Canal-Boat' which, according to J. R. Mellow, presents a 'devastating sketch' (54) of the American woman but which also presents as devastating a sketch of Hawthorne's persecutory attitude towards women. In addition, a number of the tales discuss the relationship of women to learning and education: among them, 'The Birth-mark' and 'Rappaccini's Daughter'. Several tales deal with the witchcraft era in American history: 'Young Goodman Brown', 'Alice Doane's Appeal', 'The Hollow of the Three Hills', 'The Prophetic Pictures', 'Edward Randolph's Portrait', 'Drowne's Wooden Image', for example. According to the feminist critic, N. Baym, a number of the tales uncover the psychopathology of the rejection of women, or of the feminine—'Rappaccini's Daughter', 'The Birth-mark', 'Wakefield', 'The Man of Adamant', 'The Prophetic Pictures', 'Roger Malvin's Burial', 'Young Goodman Brown', 'The Minister's Black Veil', 'The Shaker Bridal'.

For illuminating discussions of the tales, see N. Baym, 'Hawthorne's women'; M. D. Bell, *Hawthorne and the Historical Romance of New England*; C. M. Bensick, *La Nouvelle Béatrice*; F. Crews, *The Sins of the Fathers*; J. Fetterley, *The Resisting Reader* (on 'The Birth-mark'); J. R. Mellow, *Nathaniel Hawthorne*; N. F. Doubleday, *Hawthorne's Early Tales*.

4. J. D. Crowley, 'Historical commentary' to *Twice-Told Tales, The Centenary Edition of the Works of Nathaniel Hawthorne*, p. 497.
5. R. Stewart, *Nathaniel Hawthorne*, p. 79. *See* G. C. Erlich, *Family Themes and Hawthorne's Fiction*.
6. H. H. Hoeltje, 'The writing of *The Scarlet Letter*', p. 342; N. Baym, 'Nathaniel Hawthorne and his mother', pp. 20, 21. For a discussion of the effect of his mother's death on the creation of the novel, see, especially, N. Baym and G. C. Erlich. See my discussion of N. Baym's work in chapter two.
7. N. Baym, p. 1. *See* G. C. Erlich for a discussion of how his mother's death freed him to write his masterpiece.
8. L. H. Tharp, *The Peabody Sisters of Salem*, p. 190.
9. H. H. Hoeltje, p. 344.
10. W. Charvat, 'Introduction to *The Scarlet Letter*', *The Scarlet Letter, The Centenary Edition of the Works of Nathaniel Hawthorne*, p. xxii. Citations from this edition will be placed within parentheses throughout this chapter.
11. C. Ryskamp, 'The New England sources of *The Scarlet Letter*, p. 269.
12. W. Charvat, p. xxvi.
13. W. Charvat, p. xxvii. An entry in Hawthorne's *The American Notebooks* for 28 August 1837 details a visit to Eben Hathorne, who might have been the model for Surveyor Pue:

    > The pride of ancestry seems to be his great hobby; he had a good many old papers in his desk at the custom-house, which he produced and dissertated upon, and afterwards went with me to his sister's in Howard place; and showed me an old book, with a record of the first emigrants (who came over 200 years ago) children in his own handwriting. . . . As we walked, he kept telling stories of the family. . . . (74)

    An entry for 15 June 1838 describes going to the burial-ground in Charter Street, and seeing a gravestone 'to the memory of "Colonel John Hathorne, Esq.," who died in 1717. This was the witch-judge. . . . Other Hathornes lie buried in a range with him on either side' (172). Hawthorne concludes: 'It gives strange ideas, to think how convenient to Dr. Peabody's family this burial-ground is,—the monuments standing almost within arm's reach of the side windows of the parlor' (172). In my judgement, Nathaniel's marriage to Sophia Peabody was, in part, an attempt to forge a connection with his own past, and I use, as evidence, this quotation from his diaries.
14. V. Loggins, *The Hawthornes*, pp. 130–3.
15. J. Marcus has used the term in reference to Virginia Woolf's process of composition in *The Years*. *See* J. Marcus, '*The Years* as Greek drama, domestic novel, and Götterdämmerung'.

16. *See* T. W. Herbert, 'Little Pearl and Hawthorne's daughter'. Hawthorne's entries in *The American Notebooks* from 19 March 1848 to 30 July 1849 are illuminating, as Herbert argues brilliantly in his article. *See, especially*: 'The children have been playing ball together; and Una, heated by the violence with which she plays, sits down on the floor, and complains grievously of warmth—opens her breast. This is the physical manifestation of the evil spirit that struggles for the mastery of her; he is not a spirit at all, but an earthy monster, who lays his grasp on her spinal marrow, her brain, and other parts of her body that lie in closest contiguity to her soul; so that the soul has the discredit of evil deeds' (420–1). It seems bizarre to see the spectacle of the devil inhabiting one's daughter as she undoes her clothes because she has been playing with gusto.
17. V. Loggins, p. 69.

Chapter Five The House of the Seven Gables (1851)

1. W. Charvat, Introduction to *The House of the Seven Gables, The Centenary Edition of the Works of Nathaniel Hawthorne*, vol. II, p. xv. Citations to this edition will be placed within parentheses throughout the chapter.
2. W. Charvat, Introduction to *The Scarlet Letter, The Centenary Edition of the Works of Nathaniel Hawthorne*, p. xvi.
3. J. R. Mellow, *Nathaniel Hawthorne in His Times*, p. 315.
4. W. Charvat, Introduction to *The House of the Seven Gables*, p. xv.
5. J. R. Mellow, pp. 315, 314.
6. J. R. Mellow, pp. 337, 336, 333. Mellow's analysis of the language of Melville's review as being 'embarrassingly erotic' is extremely insightful. *See* J. R. Mellow, pp. 334 and following. *See also* B. Jones, 'Some "Mosses" from the *Literary World*'. Neither left a record of their first meeting, but in a letter to Horatio Bridge, Hawthorne wrote, 'I met Melville, the other day, and liked him so much that I have asked him to spend a few days with me before leaving these parts' (J. R. Mellow, p. 333).
7. J. R. Mellow, p. 317.
8. W. Charvat, Introduction to *The House of the Seven Gables*, p. xvi.
9. W. Charvat, Introduction to *The Scarlet Letter*, p. xxiv–xxv. *See also* W. Charvat, Introduction to *The House of the Seven Gables*, p. xxii.
10. W. Charvat, Introduction to *The House of the Seven Gables*, p. xxii.
11. *See* G. Erlich *Family Themes and Hawthorne's Fiction*, L. H. Tharp, *The Peabody Sisters of Salem*, J. R. Mellow, *Nathaniel Hawthorne in His Times*, and N. Hawthorne, *The American Notebooks, The Centenary Edition of the Works of Nathaniel Hawthorne*, vol. VIII, p. 429.

12. In actuality, this curse was pronounced by Goody Good to Reverend Nicholas Noyes, but legend held otherwise. *See* V. Loggins, *The Hawthornes*, p. 133.
13. A. Dworkin, *Woman Hating*, p. 130. For provocative analyses of the Salem witchcraft trials, see P. Boyer and S. Nissenbaum, *Salem Possessed* and C. W. Upham, *Salem Witchcraft*.
14. P. Boyer and S. Nissenbaum, pp. 31, 33. Boyer and Nissenbaum approach the trials as an example of a complex confluence of social and economic factors. They state that the trials were 'the most severe challenge to confront the judicial system of Massachusetts during the entire colonial period' (p. 6) but that the records of the proceedings of 1692 act as 'testament to the magistrates' efforts to seek out proofs that would conform to the established rules of courtroom evidence— ... that was empirically verifiable and logically relevant' (p. 11). Their conclusion is difficult to uphold, given a careful examination of the transcriptions provided in C. W. Upham, where Judge Hathorne lies to one of the accused. None the less, their account is a fascinating recreation of the history of Salem in changing and upsetting times, and their careful scrutiny of the sociological factors which were involved in the patterns of who were the accused and who were the accusers is compelling.

    It is interesting to note that the issue of the economic fate of women, an important issue in *The House of the Seven Gables*, surfaces again and again in the history of the trials. What triggered the episode was that a number of adolescent girls were using magic, probably learned from an Indian slave, Tituba, to try to determine whom they would marry, and, according to the testimony, 'what trade their sweethearts should be of' (p. 1), a matter of no small importance in a community which was depressed economically. One of the accused women was an outcast, like Phoebe, who had to beg for shelter; another of the accused women was elderly, like Hepzibah.
15. P. Boyer and A. Nissenbaum, p. 33.
16. *See* V. Loggins, p. 120, P. Boyer and S. Nissenbaum, p. 5.
17. M. Cronin, 'Hawthorne on romantic love and the status of women', pp. 97–8.
18. J. R. Mellow, pp. 294–5, 300, 302.
19. C. W. Upham, *Salem Witchcraft*. Although this monumental volume, which included transcriptions from the trial, did not appear until 1867, Upham had published, in 1831, *Lectures on Witchcraft*. Both were based upon lectures that Upham had delivered.
20. C. W. Upham, pp. 13–17.
21. C. W. Upham, p. 59. Upham reproduces the text of the document signed by Elizabeth Porter. The accused woman was Rebecca Nurse, a great-grandmother, described by Upham as a good, church-going woman, who was an invalid at the time of the accusation. Upham describes Hathorne's 'line of criminating questions' (p. 66).

22. J. R. Mellow, p. 302.
23. J. R. Mellow, p. 361.
24. F. Bowers in his Textual Introduction to *The House of the Seven Gables*, p. xxxvii, observes that in the Harvard manuscript of the novel, Hawthorne has made the 'thorough-going alteration of the references to Hepzibah as "the Old Maid"' and has substituted her name. According to L. H. Tharp in *The Peabody Sisters of Salem*, p. 195, Hepzibah is a composite portrait of the Hawthorne women who were 'utterly incapable of earning a living—while at the same time anxious to try'.
25. For useful discussions of housekeeping, see R. S. Cowan, *More Work for Mother* and J. Finch and D. Groves, eds, *A Labour of Love*.
26. For an illuminating discussion of Holgrave as reformer, see N. Baym's chapter on *The House of the Seven Gables* in *The Shape of Hawthorne's Career*.
27. N. Baym, *The Shape of Hawthorne's Career*.

Chapter Six The Blithedale Romance (1852)

1. J. R. Mellow, *Nathaniel Hawthorne in His Times* p. 388.
2. L. H. Tharp, *The Peabody Sisters of Salem*, pp. 169, 189, 225. While in Washington, Mary Mann met Lucretia Mott, colleague of Elizabeth Cady Stanton.
3. H. H. Hoeltje, *Inward Sky*, p. 367.
4. It is unlikely that he began the work until after 23 November, and he recorded that he wrote 'the last page' on 30 April 1852, afterwards writing the preface and modifying the conclusion by adding the chapter in which Miles Coverdale, the narrator, declares his unrequited love for Priscilla. The novel had taken him five months to write. (J. R. Mellow, p. 388); R. H. Pearce, Introduction to *The Blithedale Romance*, pp. xvii–xviii. *See also*, N. Hawthorne's 'Preface' to the romance, in which he states that 'many readers will probably suspect a faint and not very faithful shadowing of Brook Farm', admits that he has availed himself of his 'actual reminiscences, in the hope of giving a more lifelike tint to the fancy-sketch in the following pages' but disclaims any one-to-one correspondence between members of the community and his characters, referring to them instead as 'creatures of his brain', and as 'imaginary progeny' (p. 2). All further page references are to this edition and will be placed in parentheses with the text.

   George Ripley 'formulated the motives [of the community]: "Our objects, as you know, are to insure a more natural union between intellectual and manual labor than now exists; to combine the thinker and the worker, as far as possible, in the same individual"' (T. Stoehr, 'Art vs. Utopia', p. 91). *See also*, J. T. Codman, *Brook Farm*.

5. N. Hawthorne, *The American Notebooks*, p. 209.
6. N. Hawthorne, *The American Notebooks*, p. 202.
7. J. T. Codman, p. 8; L. Swift, *Brook Farm*, p. 164.
8. N. Hawthorne, *Love Letters of Nathaniel Hawthorne*, p. 7.
9. L. Swift, p. 166.
10. N. Hawthorne, *Love Letters of Nathaniel Hawthorne*, p. 32.
11. A. Turner, Introduction to *The Blithedale Romance*, p. 8.
12. L. Swift, p. 170. According to the contemporary account of J. T. Codman, p. 20, Hawthorne had to perform manual labour because he was 'the most simple-minded of all men in matters of ordinary business, . . . and unwilling to act as teacher', the two other forms of work available to him.
13. In 'Years of experience', quoted by J. T. Codman, p. 21.
14. R. H. Pearce, Introduction to the Centenary Edition of *The Blithedale Romance*, p. xxv.
15. *See*, for example, I. Howe, *Politics and the Novel*: 'Coverdale is a self-portrait of Hawthorne, but a highly distorted and mocking self-portrait' (166).

    Mitchell A. Leaska, in *Virginia Woolf's Lighthouse*, has this to say about the narrator of Henry James's *The Sacred Fount*, a narrator very much like Coverdale:

    > when the reader has no way of knowing about the narrator except from the process of his 'acting himself out', there is apt to be trouble. . . . As a result, the reader is to the very end helplessly confined to only the evidence which the narrator chooses to furnish . . . [W]e are at a loss as to how credible a witness he is. It takes no profound analysis to discover that the narrator is given to flights of fantasy; that he keeps a good deal of emotional distance between himself and others. . . . The reader . . . discovers at the end that nothing has been solved; in fact, nothing has actually happened that needs to be solved except for evaluating the narrator's ornate and highly suspect ruminations.

    See M.A. Leaska, pp. 35–6.

    The views in this essay have been developed from an earlier exploration of the subject. *See* L. A. DeSalvo, 'John Gardner's drama of power'.
16. In fact, at Brook Farm, the women did all the housework: 'The usual duties were mainly discharged by the young women, no attempt being made to foist on the men tasks beyond their experience or knowledge' (L. Swift, *Brook Farm*, p. 50). For a brilliant analysis of an alternative strategy used by women to gain power by downplaying the earlier interpretation of them as carnal, see N. F. Cott, 'Passionlessness'.

17. The homosexual theme is developed on pp. 133, 135, 138, 143, 145, 146, 153. G. C. Erlich, in *Family Themes and Hawthorne's Fiction* reads the Coverdale/Hollingsworth relationship as central to the novel's thematic development. She disagrees with those critics who believe that Melville was the inspiration for the Hollingsworth character, stating that in the Hawthorne/Melville relationship, Hawthorne was the older, more respected man and Melville the young man seeking the older man's favour. Erlich believes that the Coverdale/Hollingsworth relationship is another in the numerous male relationships in Hawthorne's fiction in which Hawthorne's early experience with his uncle is the source for the emotional configurations of these scenes. *See* G. C. Erlich, pp. 129–31.
18. If one wished to pursue this line of argument, it should be noted that Coverdale begins chapter XXII, where he discusses Moodie's past, by stating that 'Five-and-twenty years ago, at the epoch of this story, there dwelt, in one of the middle states, a man whom we shall call Fauntleroy.' C. Swann, in 'A note on *The Blithedale Romance*, or "Call him Fauntleroy"', points out that the historical Fauntleroy was a man who, legend held, had managed to escape the death penalty for a crime. It might be argued that the real Fauntleroy figure in the novel is Coverdale and not Moodie.
19. *See* B. G. Chevigny, 'The long arm of censorship', p. 451: 'Fuller was endorsing with growing fervor that early eclectic socialist thought stemming from Fourier which liberated sexuality, banished gender stereotyping, and reshaped family structure as well as restoring dignity to labor.' *See also*, Margaret Fuller [Ossoli], *Woman in the Nineteenth Century*; A. Douglas, 'Margaret Fuller and the disavowal of fiction' in *The Feminization of American Culture*; and M. Wade, *Margaret Fuller*.

Epilogue

1. See S. Cameron's brilliant analysis of the form of the romance in *The Corporeal Self*.

Select Bibliography

Arvin, N., Introduction to *Hawthorne's Short Stories* (Vintage, New York, 1946).

Auerbach, N., *Woman and the Demon: The Life of a Victorian Myth* (Harvard University Press, Cambridge, Massachusetts and London, 1982).

Baylor, R. M. *Elizabeth Palmer Peabody: Kindergarten Pioneer* (University of Pennsylvania Press, Philadelphia, 1965).

Baym, N. 'Hawthorne's gothic discards: *Fanshawe* and "Alice Doane"', *Nathaniel Hawthorne Journal*, 4 (1974), pp. 105–15.

——, 'Hawthorne's women: the tyranny of social myths', *The Centennial Review* 15:3 (Summer 1971), pp. 250–72.

——, 'Melodramas of beset manhood: how theories of American fiction exclude women authors', *American Quarterly*, 33:2 (Summer 1981), pp. 123–39.

——, 'Nathaniel Hawthorne and his mother: a biographical speculation', *American Literature*, 54:1 (March 1982), pp. 1–27.

——, 'Passion and authority in *The Scarlet Letter*', *The New England Quarterly*, 43:2 (June 1970), pp. 209–30.

——, 'The Romantic *Malgré lui*: Hawthorne in the Custom House', *ESQ*, 19:1 (first quarter 1973), pp. 14–25.

——, *The Shape of Hawthorne's Career* (Cornell University Press, Ithaca and London, 1976).

——, 'The significance of plot in Hawthorne's romances', in *Ruined Eden of the Present*, ed G. R. Thompson and V. L. Lokke, (Purdue University Press, West Lafayette, Indiana, 1981), pp. 49–70.

——, *Women's Fiction: a Guide to Novels by and about Women in America, 1820–1870* (Cornell University Press, Ithaca and London, 1978).

Bell, M., *Hawthorne's View of the Artist* (State University of New York, New York, 1962).

Bell, M. D. *The Development of American Romance: The Sacrifice of Relation* (Chicago University Press, Chicago and London, 1980).

——, *Hawthorne and the Historical Romance of New England* (Princeton University Press, Princeton, New Jersey, 1971).

Bensick, C. M. *La Nouvelle Béatrice: Renaissance and romance in 'Rappaccini's Daughter'* (Rutgers University Press, New Brunswick, 1985).

Berryman, C. *From Wilderness to Wasteland: The Trial of the Puritan God in the American Imagination* (National University Publications, Kennikat Press, Port Washington, N.Y., 1979).

Bicknell, J. W. '*The Marble Faun* reconsidered', *University of Kansas City Review*, XX (Spring 1954), pp. 193–9.

Bode, C. 'Hawthorne's *Fanshawe*: the promising of greatness', *The New England Quarterly, A Historical Review of New England Life and Letters*, 23:2 (June 1950), pp. 235–2.

Bowers, F. Textual Introduction to the Centenary Edition of *The Blithedale Romance* (Ohio State University Press, Columbus, 1964).

Boyer P. and Nissenbaum, S. *Salem Possessed: The Social Origins of Witchcraft* (Harvard University Press, Cambridge, Massachusetts, 1974).

Caldwell, W. T. 'The emblem tradition and the symbolic mode; clothing imagery in *The House of the Seven Gables*, *ESQ*, 19:1 (first quarter 1973), pp. 34–42.

Cameron, S. *The Corporeal Self: Allegories of the Body in Melville and Hawthorne* (Johns Hopkins University Press, Baltimore and London, 1981).

Cantwell, R. *Nathaniel Hawthorne: The American Years* (Octagon, New York, 1971, reprint of New York, Holt, Rinehart & Winston, 1949 edition).

Carpenter, F. I. 'Scarlet A minus', *College English*, 5:4 (January 1944), pp. 173–80.

Charvat, W. *The Profession of Authorship in America, 1800–1870* (Ohio State University Press, Columbus, 1964).

Chevigny, B. G. 'The long arm of censorship: mythmaking in Margaret Fuller's time and our own', *Signs*, 2:2 (Winter 1976), pp. 450–60.

Christ, C. 'Victorian masculinity and the angel in the house', in *A Widening Sphere: Changing Roles of Victorian Women*, ed M. Vicinus (Indiana University Press, Bloomington and London, 1977), pp. 146–62.

Cifelli, E. 'Hawthorne as humorist: A look at *Fanshawe*', *CEA Critic*, 38:4 (May 1976), pp. 11–17.

Codman, J. T. *Brook Farm: Historic and Personal Memoirs* (AMS, New York, [1971], reprint of Arena, Boston, Mass., 1894 edition).

Colacurcio, M. J. 'Footsteps of Ann Hutchinson: the context of *The Scarlet Letter*', *ELH*, 39:3 (September 1972), pp. 459–94.

Cott, N. F. 'Passionlessness: an interpretation of Victorian sexual ideology, 1790–1850', *Signs*, 4:2 (Winter 1978), pp. 219–36.

Cowan, R. S. *More Work for Mother: The Ironies of Household Technology from the Open Hearth to the Microwave* (Basic Books, New York, 1985).

Crews, F. C., *The Sins of the Fathers: Hawthorne's Psychological Themes* (Oxford University Press, New York, 1966).

Cronin, M. 'Hawthorne on romantic love and the status of women', *PMLA*, 69:1 (March 1954), pp. 88–98.

Crowley, J. D. ed., *Hawthorne: The Critical Heritage* (Routledge & Kegan Paul, London, 1970).

Daly, M. *Beyond God the Father: Toward a Philosophy of Women's Liberation* (Beacon, Boston, 1973).

Davenport, B. Foreword to *The Scarlet Letter* (Dodd, Mead, New York, 1948).

Davidson, C. N. 'The marketing of taste': review of J. P. Tompkins, *Sensational Designs: The Cultural Work of American Fiction, 1790–1860,* (Oxford University Press, New York and London, 1985) *Vogue*, June 1985, p. 152.

——, 'Mothers and daughters in the fiction of the New Republic', in *The Lost Tradition: Mothers and Daughters in Literature*, ed C. N. Davidson and E. M. Broner, (Frederick Ungar, New York, 1980), pp. 115–127.

Davidson C. N. and Broner, E. M. eds, *The Lost Tradition: Mothers and Daughters in Literature* (Frederick Ungar, New York, 1980).

DeSalvo, L. A. 'John Gardner's drama of power: *October Light*', in *John Gardner: True Art, Moral Art*, ed B. Mendez-Egle and J. M. Haule, Living Author Series No. 5 (Pan American University, Edinburg, Texas, 1983).

——, 'Literature and sexuality: teaching the truth about the body', *Media and Methods*, 15:10 (September 1979), pp. 33, 64–7.

——, "'An earthly story with a hellish meaning": still another look at Hester Prynne', *Media and Methods* 16:8 (April 1980), p. 37.

Dillingham, W. B. 'Structure and theme in *The House of the Seven Gables, Nineteenth-Century Fiction*, 14:1 (June 1959), pp. 59–70.

Dinnerstein, D. *The Mermaid and the Minotaur* (Harper, Colophon, New York, 1977).

Doubleday, N. F. *Hawthorne's Early Tales, A Critical Study* (Duke University Press, Durham, North Carolina, 1972).

——, 'Hawthorne's Hester and feminism,' *PMLA*, 54:3 (September 1939), pp. 825–8.

Douglas, A. *The Feminization of American Culture* (Knopf, New York, 1978).

Dworkin, A. *Woman Hating* (E. P. Dutton, New York, 1974).

Ellmann, M. *Thinking About Women* (Harcourt, Brace & World, New York, 1968).

Epstein, B. 'Family, sexual morality, and popular movements in turn-of-the-century America', in *Powers of Desire: The Politics of Sexuality*, eds A. Snitow, *et al.*, pp. 117–30.

Erlich, G. C. *Family Themes and Hawthorne's Fiction: The Tenacious Web* (Rutgers University Press, New Brunswick, New Jersey, 1984).

Fetterley, J. *The Resisting Reader: A Feminist Approach to American Fiction* (Indiana University Press, Bloomington and London, 1978).

Fiedler, L. A. *Love and Death in the American Novel*, revised edition, (Dell, New York, 1966).

Finch, J. and Groves, D. eds, *A Labour of Love: Women, Work and Caring* (Routledge & Kegan Paul, Boston and London, 1983).

Flexner, E., *Century of Struggle: The Women's Rights Movement in the United States* (Harvard University Press, Cambridge, 1975).

Fogle, R. H. *Hawthorne's Fiction: The Light and The Dark* (University of Oklahoma Press, Norman, 1964).

Franzosa, J. '"The Custom-House," *The Scarlet Letter*, and Hawthorne's separation from Salem', *ESQ: A Journal of the American Renaissance*, 24:2 (Second quarter 1978), pp. 57–71.

French, M. *Shakespeare's Division of Experience* (Summit, New York, 1981).

Fryer, J. *The Faces of Eve: Women in the Nineteenth Century American Novel* (Oxford University Press, New York, 1976).

Fuller, M. [Ossoli], *Woman in the Nineteenth Century, and Kindred Papers Relating to the Sphere, Condition, and Duties of Woman*, ed A. B. Fuller, (Greenwood, New York, 1968; originally published by Roberts, Boston, 1864).

——, *The Writings of Margaret Fuller*, selected and edited by M. Wade (Augustus M. Kelley, Clifton, 1973).

Gilbert, S. M. and Gubar, S. *The Madwoman in the Attic: The Woman Writer and the Nineteenth-Century Literary Imagination* (Yale University Press, New Haven and London, 1979).

Goldstein, J. S. 'The literary source of Hawthorne's *Fanshawe*', *Modern Language Notes*, LX:1 (January 1945), pp. 1–8.

Gollin, R. K. *Portraits of Nathaniel Hawthorne* (Northern Illinois University Press, De Kalb, Illinois, 1983).

Gornick V. and Moran, B. K. eds, *Woman in Sexist Society: Studies in Power and Powerlessness* (Basic, New York and London, 1971).

Gross, R. E. 'Hawthorne's first novel: the future of a style', *PMLA*, 7–8:1 (March 1963), pp. 60–8.

Gross, S. L. '"Rappaccini's Daughter" and the nineteenth-century physician', in *Ruined Eden of the Present*, eds G. R. Thompson and V. L. Lokke, pp. 129–42.

Hartmann, H. I., 'The family as the locus of gender, class, and political struggle: the example of housework,' *Signs*, 6:3 (Spring 1981), 366–94.

Hawthorne, J. *Nathaniel Hawthorne and His Wife: A Biography*, 2 vols. (James R. Osgood, Boston, 1855, republished Scholarly, Grosse Pointe, Michigan, 1968).

Hawthorne, N. *The American Notebooks, The Centenary Edition of the Works of Nathaniel Hawthorne*, vol. VIII (Ohio State University Press, Ohio, 1972).

——, *The Blithedale Romance, The Centenary Edition of the Works of Nathaniel Hawthorne*, vol. III (Ohio State University Press, Ohio, 1964).

——, *The Complete Writings of Nathaniel Hawthorne*, vol. XVII, *Miscellanies* (Houghton Mifflin, Boston, 1900).

——, *Fanshawe, The Centenary Edition of the Works of Nathaniel Hawthorne*, vol. III (Ohio State University Press, Ohio, 1964).

——, *Hawthorne's Short Stories*, ed Newton Arvin (Vintage, New York, 1946).
——, *The House of the Seven Gables, The Centenary Edition of the Works of Nathaniel Hawthorne*, vol. II (Ohio State University Press, Ohio, 1965).
——, *Love Letters of Nathaniel Hawthorne 1839–1863*, 2 vols. (privately printed, The Society of the Dofobs, Chicago, 1907; reprinted by Microcard, with a Foreword by C. E. Frazer Clark, Jr., 1972).
——, *The Marble Faun: Or, The Romance of Monte Beni, The Centenary Edition of the Works of Nathaniel Hawthorne*, vol. IV (Ohio State University Press, Ohio, 1968).
——, *Mosses from an Old Manse, The Centenary Edition of the Works of Nathaniel Hawthorne*, vol. X (Ohio State University Press, Ohio, 1974).
——, 'Mrs. Hutchinson', in *The Complete Writings of Nathaniel Hawthorne: Miscellanies: Biographical and Other Sketches and Letters* vol. XVII, (Houghton Mifflin, Boston, 1900).
——, *The Scarlet Letter, The Centenary Edition of the Works of Nathaniel Hawthorne*, vol. I (Ohio State University Press, Ohio, 1962).
——, *The Snow-Image and Uncollected Tales, The Centenary Edition of the Works of Nathaniel Hawthorne*, vol. XI (Ohio State University Press, Ohio, 1974).
——, *Twice-Told Tales, The Centenary Edition of the Works of Nathaniel Hawthorne*, vol. IX (Ohio State University Press, Ohio, 1974).
——, *Twenty Days with Julian and Little Bunny:* A Diary (thirty copies only privately printed from the original manuscript, S. H. Wakeman, New York, 1904), Berg Collection of English and American Literature.
'Nathaniel Hawthorne', in *Nineteenth-Century Literature Criticism: Excerpts from Criticism of the Works of Novelists, Poets, Playwrights, Short Story Writers, and Other Creative Writers Who Lived between 1800 and 1900, from the First Published Critical Appraisals to Current Evaluations*, vol. 2, L. L. Harris, ed. (Gale, Detroit, Michigan, 1982).
Heilbrun, C. G. *Toward a Recognition of Androgyny* (Knopf, New York, 1973).
Herbert, T. W. 'Little Pearl and Hawthorne's daughter: an essay in the poetics of culture', unpublished essay.
——, 'Numinous mates: Nathaniel Hawthorne and the socialization of domestic intimacy', unpublished essay.

Herman, J. L. with Hirschman, L. *Father-Daughter Incest* (Harvard University Press, Cambridge, Massachusetts and London, 1981).

Hoeltje, H. H. *Inward Sky: The Mind and Heart of Nathaniel Hawthorne* (Duke University Press, Durham, North Carolina, 1962).

——, 'The writing of *The Scarlet Letter*', *The New England Quarterly*, XXVII: 3 (September 1954), pp. 326–46.

Homberger, E., 'Nathaniel Hawthorne and the dream of happiness', in *Nathaniel Hawthorne: New Critical Essays*, ed. A. Robert Lee (Vision and Barnes and Noble, Totowa, New Jersey, 1982), pp. 171–86.

Howe, I. *Politics and the Novel* (New York, Meridian, World, 1957).

Janeway, E. '"Who is Sylvia?" On the loss of sexual paradigms', *Signs*, 5:4 (Summer, 1980), pp. 573–89.

Janssen, J. G. '*Fanshawe* and Hawthorne's developing comic sense', *Emerson Society Quarterly*, 22 (1976), pp. 24–7.

Johnson, C. D. *The Productive Tension of Hawthorne's Art* (University of Alabama Press, Alabama, 1981).

Johnson, S. *The History of Rasselas, Prince of Abyssinia*, edited with an Introduction by G. Tillotson and B. Jenkins (Oxford University Press, New York and London, 1971).

Jones, B. 'Some "Mosses" from the *Literary World*: critical and bibliographical survey of the Hawthorne–Melville relationship', in *Ruined Eden of the Present*, pp. 173–203.

Justus, J. H. 'Hawthorne's Coverdale: character and art in *The Blithedale Romance*', in *American Literature*, 47:1 (March 1975–January 1976), pp. 21–36.

Kelley, M. *Private Woman, Public Stage: Literary Domesticity in Nineteenth-Century America* (Oxford University Press, New York and Oxford, 1984).

Klinkowitz, J. 'Hawthorne's sense of an ending', *ESQ*, 19:1 (first quarter 1973), pp. 43–9.

Kolodny, A. Introduction to Nathaniel Hawthorne's *The Blithedale Romance* (Penguin, Harmondsworth, England and New York, 1964, 1983).

——. *The Lay of the Land: Metaphor as Experience and History in American Life and Letters* (University of North Carolina Press, Chapel Hill, 1975).

Kosinski, J. 'Packaged passion', *The American Scholar*, 42:2 (Spring 1973), pp. 193–204.

Lawrence, D. H. *Studies in Classic American Literature* (Doubleday, Garden City, New York, 1951; originally published by Thomas Seltzer, 1923).

Leaska, M. A. *Virginia Woolf's Lighthouse: A Study in Critical Method* (Hogarth, London, 1970).

Lee, A. R. ed., *Nathaniel Hawthorne: New Critical Essays* (Vision and Barnes and Noble, Totowa, New Jersey, 1982).

Lefcowitz, A. and B., 'Some rents in the veil: new light on Priscilla and Zenobia in *The Blithedale Romance*', *Nineteenth-Century Fiction*, 21:3 (December 1966), pp. 263–75.

Leverenz, D. *The Language of Puritan Feeling: An Exploration in Literature, Psychology, and Social History* (Rutgers University Press, New Brunswick, New Jersey, 1980).

——, 'Mrs. Hawthorne's headache: reading *The Scarlet Letter*', *Nineteenth-Century Fiction* 37:4 (March 1983), pp. 552–75.

Levin, H. *The Power of Blackness: Hawthorne, Poe, Melville* (Ohio State University Press, Chicago and London, 1958, 1980).

Levy, L. B. '*Fanshawe*: Hawthorne's world of images', *Studies in the Novel: Nathaniel Hawthorne Special Number*, 2:30 (Winter 1970) pp. 440–8.

Little, J. *Comedy and the Woman Writer: Woolf, Spark, and Feminism* (University of Nebraska Press, Lincoln and London, 1983).

Loggins, V., *The Hawthornes: The Story of Seven Generations of an American Family* (Greenwood, New York, 1968).

Lundblad, J. *Nathaniel Hawthorne and the Tradition of Gothic Romance* (Haskell, New York, 1946, 1964).

McPherson, H. *Hawthorne as Myth-Maker: A Study in Imagination* (University of Toronto Department of English Studies and Texts 16, Toronto, 1969).

McWalters, J. 'In defense of poor Hester', *Media and Methods*, 16:8 (April 1980), p. 36.

Male, R. R. *Hawthorne's Tragic Vision* (University of Texas, Austin, 1967).

Marcus, J. '*The Years* as Greek drama, domestic novel, and Götterdämmerung', *Bulletin of The New York Public Library*, 80:2 (Winter 1977), pp. 276–301.

Martin, T. *Nathaniel Hawthorne* (Twayne, New York, 1965).

Martin, W. 'Seduced and abandoned in the New World: the image of woman in American fiction', in *Woman in Sexist Society*, eds V. Gornick and B. K. Moran, pp. 226–39.

May, K. M. *Characters of Women in Narrative Literature* (St Martin's, New York, 1981).

Mellow, J. R. *Nathaniel Hawthorne in His Times* (Houghton Mifflin, Boston, 1980).

Messerli, J. *Horace Mann: A Biography* (Knopf, New York, 1971).

Millett, K. *Sexual Politics* (Doubleday, Garden City, New York, 1970).

Newberry, F. 'Tradition and disinheritance in *The Scarlet Letter*', *ESQ*, 23:1 (first quarter 1977), pp. 1–26.

Pancost, D. W. 'Hawthorne's epistemology and ontology', *ESQ*, 19:1 (first quarter 1973), pp. 8–13.

Pauly, T. H. 'Hawthorne's houses of fiction', *American Literature*, 48:3 (November 1976), pp. 271–91.

Pearce, R. H. Introduction to the Centenary Edition of *The Blithedale Romance* (Ohio State University Press, Columbus, 1964).

——, Introduction to the Centenary Edition of *Fanshawe* (Ohio State University Press, Columbus, 1964).

Perry, R. *Women, Letters, and the Novel* (AMS, New York, 1980).

Petter, H. *The Early American Novel* (Ohio State University Press, Columbus, 1971).

Pleck, E. 'Feminist responses to "crimes against women", 1868–1893', *Signs*: special issue; Women and Violence, 8:3 (Spring 1983), pp. 451–70.

Pomeroy, S. B. *Goddesses, Whores, Wives, and Slaves: Women in Classical Antiquity* (Schocken, New York, 1975).

Rich, A. 'Compulsory heterosexuality and lesbian existence', in *Powers of Desire*, eds A. Snitow, *et al.*, pp. 177–205.

Ringe, D. A. 'Romantic iconology in *The Scarlet Letter* and *The Blithedale Romance*', in *Ruined Eden of the Present* eds G. R. Thompson and V. L. Lokke, pp. 93–107.

Rosa, A., *Salem, Transcendentalism, and Hawthorne* (Fairleigh Dickinson University Press, Teaneck, New Jersey and Associated University Presses, London, 1980).

Ross E. and Rapp, R. 'Sex and society; a research note from social history and anthropology', in *Powers of Desire* eds A. Snitow *et al.*, pp. 51–73.

Ryan, M. P., *Womanhood in America: From Colonial Times to the Present* (Franklin Watts, New York, 1979).

Ryskamp, C. 'The New England sources of *The Scarlet Letter*', *American Literature*, 31:3 (November 1959), pp. 257–72.

Sattelmeyer, R. 'The aesthetic background of Hawthorne's

Fanshawe', *Nathaniel Hawthorne Journal*, 5 (1975), pp. 200–9.

Schoen, C. 'House of the Seven Deadly Sins', *ESQ*, 19:1 (first quarter 1973), pp. 26–33.

Showalter, E. 'Critical cross-dressing: male feminists and the woman of the year', *Raritan*, (Autumn 1983) pp. 130–49.

Shurr, W. H. 'Eve's bower: Hawthorne's transition from public doctrines to private truths', in *Ruined Eden of the Present*, eds G. R. Thompson and V. L. Lokke, pp. 143–69.

Simpson, C. M. Introduction to the Centenary Edition of *The Marble Faun: or, The Romance of Monte Beni*.

Smith-Rosenberg, C., 'The Female World of Love and Ritual: Relations Between Women in Nineteenth-Century America', *Signs* 1:1 (Autumn 1975), pp. 1–29.

Snitow, A. B. 'Mass market romance: pornography for women is different', in *Powers of Desire*, eds A. Snitow, *et al.*, pp. 245–63.

Snitow, A., Stansell, C. and Thompson, S. eds, *Powers of Desire: The Politics of Sexuality* (Monthly Review Press, New York, 1983).

Stewart, R. *Nathaniel Hawthorne: A Biography* (Yale University Press, New Haven and London, 1948).

Stoehr, T., 'Art vs. Utopia: the case of Nathaniel Hawthorne and Brook Farm', *The Antioch Review*, 36:1 (Winter 1978), pp. 89–102.

Stouck, D. 'The Surveyor of the Custom House: a narrator for *The Scarlet Letter*', *The Centennial Review*, 15:3 (Summer 1971), pp. 309–29.

Swann, C. 'A note on *The Blithedale Romance*, or "Call him Fauntleroy"', *Journal of American Studies*, 10:1 (April 1976), pp. 103–4.

Swift, L. *Brook Farm: Its Members, Scholars, and Visitors* (Corinth, New York, 1961, reprint of 1900 edition).

Tharp, L. H. *The Peabody Sisters of Salem* (Little, Brown, Boston, 1950).

Thompson G. R. and Lokke, V. L. eds, *Ruined Eden of the Present: Hawthorne, Melville, and Poe; Critical Essays in Honor of Darrel Abel* (Purdue University Press, West Lafayette, Indiana, 1981).

Tompkins, J. P. *Sensational Designs: The Cultural Work of American Fiction, 1790–1860* (Oxford University Press, New York and London, 1985).

Turner, A. Introduction to *The Blithedale Romance* (New York, W. W. Norton, 1958).

Upham, C. W. *Salem Witchcraft; with An Account of Salem Village, and A History of Opinions on Witchcraft and Kindred Subjects*, 2 vols. (Corner House Publishers, Social Science Reprints, Williamstown, Massachusetts, 1971; originally published in 1867).

Vicinus, M. ed., *A Widening Sphere: Changing Roles of Victorian Women* (Indiana University Press, Bloomington and London, 1977).

Von Abele, R., *The Death of the Artist: A Study of Hawthorne's Disintegration* (Martinus Nijhoff, The Hague,1955).

Wade, M. *Margaret Fuller: Whetstone of Genius* (Viking, New York, 1940).

Wagenknecht, E. *Nathaniel Hawthorne: Man and Writer* (Oxford University Press, New York, 1961).

Waggoner, H. H. *Hawthorne: A Critical Study*, (Harvard University Press, Cambridge, Massachusetts, 1955, 1963, and Oxford, London, 1955, 1963, revised editions).

Walkowitz, J. R. 'Male vice and female virtue: feminism and the politics of prostitution in nineteenth-century Britain', in *Powers of Desire*, eds A. Snitow, *et al.*, pp. 419–38.

Warren, J. W. *The American Narcissus: Individualism and Women in Nineteenth-Century American Fiction* (Rutgers University Press, New Brunswick, New Jersey, 1984).

Welter, B. *Dimity Convictions: The American Woman in the Nineteenth Century* (Ohio University Press, Athens, 1976).

Young, P. *Hawthorne's Secret: An Un-Told Tale* (David R. Godine, Boston, 1984).

Index

'A', image of, 75
Abandonment, 41–3, 71, 119, 121
Abolitionist movement, 1, 16
Adultery, 63–4, 67–9, 75
Alcott, Bronson, 15
'Alice Doane's Appeal', 3
'Alice Pyncheon', 92–6
American eagle (symbol in *The Scarlet Letter*), 59–60
Ancestors, 9, 51, 56, 58, 61, 63–76, 79–84, 91–2, 96
Angels, image of women as, 5, 18, 29, 89–91
Annals of Salem (Joseph Felt), 63
Antinomians, 70, 73
Auerbach, Nina, 25, 31–2
Authority, 29, 94
Aylmer in 'The Birthmark', 26, 47

Bancroft, George, 16
Baylor, Ruth M., 15
Baym, Nina, 25, 34–5, 53, 54, 72–3, 74, 94–5, 113, 116
Beatrice (in 'Rappaccini's Daughter'), 27
Bell, Michael Davitt, 74
Bell, Millicent, 52
Biblical images, 90, 96, 105
Bicknell, John W., xiv
'Birth-mark, The,' 26, 47
Blithedale Romance, The (1852), 5, 27, 31, 34, 97–118, 120
analysis of, 99–113
and Biblical images, 105
and Brook Farm, 98–9
and current political events, 34, 97
characters in,
  Miles Coverdale, 28, 98–113, 115–18
  Hollingsworth, 97, 102–3, 108–9, 115
  Priscilla, 27, 28, 31, 98, 100, 102, 108, 115
  Zenobia, 5–6, 13, 27–8, 31, 99–113, 115
  Westervelt, 112–13, 117
criticism of, 113–16
and feminism, 5–6, 100, 104, 107
and housework, 104–5
and homosexuality, 109
and images of women, 100–18
and the metaphor of the Veiled Lady, 99–100
and misogyny, 117–18, 109–12
and psychopathology of the narrator, 109–12, 117–18
as satire, 97
and sexuality, 105–10
significance of the ending, 117–21

use of unreliable narrator, 99–118

Bode, Carl, 52

Boston Weekly Messenger, 52

Bowdoin College, xiii, 39

Boyer, Paul, 81

Bridge, Horatio, xiii, 77

Brook Farm, 34, 98–9, 115

Butler (character in *Fanshawe*), 39–42, 44, 46, 48, 51

Capitalism and women, 32, 50–1, 55–6, 84–92

Carpenter, Frederic I., 71–2

Channing, William Ellery, 16

Charvat, William, 63

Childhood

of Nathaniel Hawthorne, 2, 50–1, 56

of Pearl (character in *The Scarlet Letter*), 21, 36, 65, 69–71

sexual abuse in, 50

of Una Hawthorne, 2, 16, 18–22, 36, 70

Chillingworth (in *The Scarlet Letter*), 64–5

Cifelli, E., 54–5

Cilley, Jonathan, xiii

Clarke, Sarah, 16

Colacurcio, M. J., 73

College life (in *Fanshawe*), 39, 47–8, 53

Comedy, 50, 54–5

Coverdale in (*The Blithedale Romance*), 28, 98–113, 115–18

Creation of novels, 57–8, 60–1, 67–8, 77–80

Creativity and Elizabeth Hawthorne's (his mother's) death, 58, 72–3

Crews, Frederick, 53–4

Critic, The, 52

Criticism of Hawthorne's novels, 23–38, 51–5, 63, 71–5, 77, 94–6, 113–16

Crombie, Hugh, in *Fanshawe*, 43–4, 46, 48

Cronin, Morton, 72–82, 114

Custom-House, 57

'The Custom-House', 3, 58–61, 65–8, 70, 72–3, 75, 78–9

Davidson, Cathy, 33–4

Death,

of Nathaniel Hawthorne, 21

of Hawthorne's father, 2, 51

of Hawthorne's mother, 51, 56, 58, 72–3

Depression, 51

de Stael, Madame, 15

Difference between the sexes, 14 (*See also, entries under Women*)

Dillingham, William B., 94

Dimmesdale (in *The Scarlet Letter*), 27, 64–5, 70–2

Dinnerstein, Dorothy, 51

Doubleday, Neal Frank, 4–5, 53

Douglas, Ann, 32–3

Drayton, Daniel, 97

Dr Melmoth (in *Fanshawe*), 39–41, 42, 45–9, 53, 55

Dworkin, Andrea, 80

Education,

in *Fanshawe*, 39, 47–8, 53

of Hawthorne, xiii

and sexuality, xi–xii

Edward Walcott (in *Fanshawe*), 42–50

Ellen Langton (in *Fanshawe*), 13, 39–49, 51, 53, 55

Ellman, Mary, 54

Emerson, Ralph Waldo, 15, 16

Enculturation, literature as a form of, xi–xii, 76

'Endicott and the Red Cross', 3

Ending of the novels, meaning of, 50, 71, 78–9, 95–6, 117–18, 119–21

Erlich, Gloria C., 25, 35–6, 73, 95
Eroticism, 44, 105–6, 108–9

Fanshawe (in *Fanshawe*), 43–5, 48–51
Fanshawe, A Tale (1828), 39–56, 119–21
  and abandonment, 43, 45
  analysis of, 40–51
  and Bowdoin College, 39
  characters in,
    Butler, 39–42, 44, 46, 48, 51
    Dr Melmoth, 39–41, 42, 45–9, 53, 55
    Ellen Langton, 39–49, 51, 53, 55
    Fanshawe, 43–5, 48–51
    Hugh Crombie, 43–4, 46, 68
    Merchant Langton, 39, 42, 46, 48
    Mrs Melmoth, 40–1, 45–7, 49
    Walcott, 42–50
    Widow Butler, 43
  and college life, 39, 47–8, 53
  its critical reception, 51–2
  criticism of, 51–5
  and death of Hawthorne's father, 51
  and Elizabeth Hawthorne (his mother), 51, 56
  ending of, 50, 119–21
  and Hawthorne's reading, 53
  and images of fatherhood, 45, 51
  and images of men, 49, 51
  and images of prey, 44–7
  and images of women, 47–50, 53–4
  and male violence, 44–7, 50, 119–21
  and marriage, 39, 45–7, 53
  and misogyny, 46
  narrator in, 41
  and poverty, 50–1, 55–6
  publication of, 39–40
  and Robert Manning, 50–1
  as satire of gothic novel, 48–9, 52, 55
  as satire of sentimental novel, 45, 49–50, 55
  and sexual abuse, 50
  and Sophia Hawthorne, 40
  and suicide, 51, 53
  and tale of Merchant's Daughter, 47–8
  and widowhood, 43–4, 51–2, 55
  and witchcraft, 46
Fathers, as figures in novels, 39, 42, 45–8, 51, 70–1, 95
Fear of women, 26–7, 47
  see also Misogyny
Felt, Joseph, 63
Feminism, 107
  two waves of, 33
  see also Women
Feminist criticism of Hawthorne, 23–38
  see also under individual critics and under listings for novels
Feminists, Hawthorne's attitudes to and portraits of, 1–22, 100, 104, 107, 129–30n3
Fern, Fanny
  Ruth Hall, 14
Fetterley, Judith, 25–6, 53
Fiedler, Leslie, 53, 54
Fields, James T., 40, 77
Franzosa, John, 73
Fryer, Judith, 25, 26–7
Fuller, Margaret, 1, 10–12, 15, 16, 17

Garden of Eden myth,
  in American literature, 27, 30–1
  in Hawthorne, 90, 96, 105
Georgiana (in 'The Birthmark'), 26, 47
Gervayse Pyncheon (in *The House of the Seven Gables*), 79, 84
Gilbert, Sandra, 25, 28–31, 116
Goldstein, Jesse Sidney, 52–3
Good, Dorcas, 81

Good, Sarah, 82–3
Gubar, Susan, 25, 28–31, 116
Hale, Sarah Josepha, 32, 51
Hathorne, Captain Nathaniel (father), 2, 50–1
Hathorne, John (Puritan ancestor), 3, 67, 80, 82–3, 96
Hathorne, William (Puritan ancestor), 3, 66–7, 74
Hawthorne, Elizabeth (Ebe, his sister), 35–6, 39, 40, 79
Hawthorne, Elizabeth Clarke Manning (mother), 2, 34–5, 51, 55–6, 58, 73, 79
Hawthorne, Julian, 16, 17, 19
Hawthorne, Nathaniel
  and ancestors, 3, 9–10, 51, 56, 58, 61, 63–76, 79–84, 91–2, 96
  his childhood, 2, 50–1, 56
  his death, 21
  and feminism, 1–22, 100, 104, 107
  as husband and father, 16–22, 70
  his misogyny, xiii , 24–5, 60, 120–2,
  and his mother, 34–5, 36, 58, 73
  his popularity, 37–8
  and poverty, 57
  relationship between his life and his fiction, 35–6, 55–6, 58, 61–2, 72–3, 79
  as wage-earner, 2, 50–1
  and witchcraft trials, 66–70, 75, 79–84, 96
  his women characters, 4–6, 12–13, 27–8, 31–49, 51, 53, 55, 61–73, 75, 79, 84–94, 96, 98–113, 115
  on women as writers, 7–10
  views on the nature of women, 6–12, 21, 68–9
  views on slavery, 19–20
  For works, see under individual titles
Hawthorne, Rose, 16, 19
Hawthorne, Sophia Peabody, 2, 11, 16–22, 37, 40, 57–8, 78–9, 98
Hawthorne, Una, 2, 16, 18–22, 36, 70
Heilbrun, Carolyn G., 24, 25
Hepzibah (in *The House of the Seven Gables*), 79, 84–9
Herbert, T. Walter, 17, 20–1, 25, 36
Hester Prynne (in *The Scarlet Letter*), 4–6, 13, 24, 27, 32–4, 61–73, 75
Hibbins, Mistress (in *The Scarlet Letter*), 66, 70, 71
Hilda (in *The Marble Faun*), xiv, 27
Hintz, Caroline Lee, 14
History, 62–3, 69, 75–6, 79–84, 96
  of women, 62–4, 66–9, 79–84, 96
Hoeltje, Herbert, 113–14
Holgrave (in *The House of the Seven Gables*), 91–3, 96
Hollingsworth (in *Blithedale Romance*), 97, 102–3, 108–9, 115
Holmes, Oliver Wendell, xiii, 16, 77
Homberger, Eric, 52
Homosexuality, 50–1, 109, 136n17
House of the Seven Gables, The (1851), 3, 77–96, 119, 120
  analysis of, 79–94
  and 'Alice Pyncheon' tale, 92–6
  and ancestors, 79–84, 91–2, 96
  and attitudes to women, 87–94
  and Biblical images, 90, 96
  characters in,
    Alice Pyncheon in 'Alice Pyncheon', 92–4, 96,
    Clifford, 79, 84, 87–8, 90–2
    Colonel Pyncheon, 81
    Gervayse Pyncheon, 92–3

Hepzibah, 79, 84–9
Holgrave, 91–3, 96
Judge Pyncheon, 79, 84
Matthew Maule, 80–2
Phoebe, 87–93, 96
creation of, 77–80
criticism of, 94–6
and dispute with Charles Wentworth Upham, 82–4
ending of, 78–9, 95–6, 119–21
and housework, 89–91
and image of the angel in the house, 89–91
and image of marriage, 93, 94–6
narrator in, 85–6, 92–4
and paternal figures, 95
and reform, 91–2, 94–5
significance of the ending, 95–6, 119–21
and witchcraft trials, 79–84, 96
and women's poverty, 84–6, 88
and women's work, 86–7, 88–92
and women's history, 79–84, 96
Housework, 40–1, 89–91, 104–5
Hugh Crombie (*Fanshawe*), 43–4, 46, 68
Hutchinson, Anne, 6–10, 70, 73

Incest, 35–6, 79, 87, 88, 127n6
Individualism and American literature, 36–7
Images,
of 'A', 75
of American eagle, 59–60
of angel in the house, 89–91
of fatherhood, 45, 51, 70–1
of marriage, 93, 94–6
of men, 49, 51
of motherhood, 70–1
of prey, 44–7
of women, 47–50, 53–4, 59–60, 68–75, 100–18,

Janssen, James G., 54–5
Jewsbury, Geraldine, 1
Judge Jaffrey Pyncheon (in *The House of the Seven Gables*), 79, 84
Justus, James H., 113

Klinkowitz, Jerome, 94
Kolodny, Annette, 34, 114–15

Ladies' Magazine, 51
Langton, Ellen, in *Fanshawe*
Lawrence, D. H., xii
Lefcowitz, Allan and Barbara, 114
Leggett, William, 52
Leverenz, David, 4, 24
Literary World, 78
Little, Judy, 50
Loggins, Vernon, 67, 74–5
Longfellow, Henry Wadsworth, 16
Love, 93–6, 113

Mailer, Norman, 23
'Main Street', 3
Male violence, 44–7, 50, 109–12, 117–18, 119–21
Mann, Horace, 1, 16, 22, 97
Mann, Mary Peabody, 1, 22, 97
Manning, Richard (uncle), 2
Manning, Robert (uncle), 2, 50–1, 79, 95
Marble Faun, The (1860), xiv, 27
Marriage, 13, 17–22, 39, 45–7, 93–6
Martin, Terence, 52
Martin, Wendy, 25, 28, 115–16
Martineau, Harriet, 1, 31
Materialism, 48
Matthew Maule (*The House of the Seven Gables*), 80–2
Maturin, Charles Robert
Melmoth the Wanderer, 53
Maule, Matthew (in *The House of the Seven Gables*), 80–2
'Maypole of Merry Mount, The', 3
McLaughlin, Prof. Frank, xi
Media and Methods, xi
Mellow, James R., 53, 83, 113

Dr Melmoth (*in Fanshawe*), 39–41, 42, 45–9, 53, 55
Mrs Melmouth (in *Fanshawe*), 40–1, 45–7, 49
Melville, Herman, 77–8
Men
  attitude to women, xii
  characters, 28, 39–51, 53, 55, 61–2, 64–5, 68, 70–2, 79–82, 84, 87–8, 90–3, 96–113, 115–18
  fear of women, 26–7, 47
  and nature, 5
  as novelists, 23–33, 62
  perception of women, 102
  responsibility for their behaviour, 47, 60, 65
  rewriting women's history, 62–4, 66–9, 79–84, 96
  and violence, 44–7, 50, 119–21
'Merchant's Daughter', tale of, 47–8
Merchant Langton (in *Fanshawe*), 39, 42, 46, 48
Miles Coverdale (in *Blithedale Romance*), 28, 98–113, 115–18
Miller, Henry, 23
Millett, Kate, 2, 23–4
Miriam (in *The Marble Faun*), xiv, 13, 27
Misogyny, xiii, 4, 23–5, 29, 46, 60, 91, 99, 109–12, 114, 117–18, 120–2
Mistress Hibbins (in *The Scarlet Letter*), 66, 70, 71
Moby Dick (Herman Melville), 77–8
Monsters, women as, 30, 46
Mosses from an Old Manse, 57
Motherhood, 32–4, 70–1
'Mrs Hutchinson', 6–10
Myths of Western culture, 24, 26–7, 37, 55

Narrators, 41, 85–6, 92–4
Newberry, Frederick, 73–4
New England Galaxy, 52
Nissenbaum, Stephen, 81

Old Testament, xiv, 27, 90, 96, 105

Pancost, D. W., 94
Paradise, 71
Paternal figures, 95
Patmore, Coventry, 5
Patriarchy, 4, 23, 68, 122
Peabody, Elizabeth, 1, 14–16, 19–20, 79
Peabody, Sophia, 2, 11, 16–22, 37, 40, 57–8, 78–9, 98
Pearl, (in *The Scarlet Letter*), 21, 36, 65, 69–71
Perry, Ruth, 31
Persecution,
  of adultery, 63–4, 67–9, 75
  of Anne Hutchinson, 6–10, 70, 73
  of witches, 66–70, 75
Phoebe (in *The House of the Seven Gables*), 87–93, 96
Pierce, Franklin, xiii, 97
Pike, William, 98
Porter, Elizabeth, 83
Poverty, 2–3, 43, 50–1, 55–6, 84–6
Powerlessness, 50–1, 96, 101, 119–21
Priscilla (in *Blithedale Romance*), 27, 28, 31, 98, 100, 102, 108, 115
Prynne, Hester (in *The Scarlet Letter*), 4, 27, 32–4, 61–73, 75
Psychopathology of narrator in *Blithedale Romance*, 109–12, 117–18
Pue, Surveyor Johathan (in *The Scarlet Letter*), 61–2
Pyncheon, Alice (in *The House of the Seven Gables*), 92–4, 96
Pyncheon, Colonel, (in *The House*

of the Seven Gables), 81
Pyncheon, Gervayse, in (*The House of the Seven Gables*), 92–3
Pyncheon, Judge Jaffrey, in (*The House of the Seven Gables*), 79, 84
Puritanism, xii, 3–4, 10, 61, 63–76, 73–6
Pyncheons (in *The House of the Seven Gables*), 79, 81, 84, 92–3

Quakers, 66–7

'Rappaccini's Daughter', 27
Reform, 65, 91–2, 94–5, 97, 104
'Resisting reader' approach of Judith Fetterley, 25–6
Responsibility for men, 47, 60, 65
Roger Chillingworth (in *The Scarlet Letter*), 64–5
Romance, 48–50, 54, 120
Rosa, Alfred, 113
Ryscamp, Charles, 63
Ruth Hall (Fanny Fern), 14

Salem Gazette, 6, 57
Salem witchcraft trials, 3, 46, 66–70, 74–5, 79–84
Satire, 45, 48–50, 52, 55, 97
Sattelmeyer, Robert, 52–3
Scarlet Letter, The (1850), 1, 3, 4–6, 24, 28, 33, 52, 57–76, 119, 120
  and adultery, 63–4, 67–9, 75
  and Anne Hutchinson, 70, 73, 74
  and American dream, 72
  analysis of, 58–71
  and ancestors, 66–7, 72–6
  characters in
    Chillingworth, 64–5
    Dimmesdale, 64–5, 70–2
    Hester Prynne, 4, 27, 32–4, 61–73, 75
    Mistress Hibbins, 66, 70, 71
    Pearl, 21, 36, 65, 69–71
    Surveyor Jonathan Pue, 61–2
  and contemporary politics, 58–9, 65–5
  creation of, 57–8, 60–1, 67–8
  criticism of, 63, 71–5, 77
  and Custom-House, 57
  'The Custom-House', 58–61, 65–8, 70, 72–3, 75, 78, 79
  and Elizabeth Manning Hawthorne's (his mother's) death, 58, 72–3
  and enculturation, xi–xii, 76
  form of, 60–4
  and image of the American eagle, 59–60
  and image of fatherhood, 70–1
  and image of the letter 'A', 75
  and image of motherhood, 70–1
  and images of women, 59–60, 68–75
  and persecution of adultery, 63–4, 67–9, 75
  and persecution of witches, 66–70, 75
  publication of, 1
  and Puritan New England, 61, 63–71, 73–6
  significance of the ending, 71, 119–21
  and social reform, 65
  and Sophia Hawthorne, 57–8
  and Una Hawthorne, 70
  and women's history, 62–4, 66–9
Schoen, Carl, 95
Scott, Sir Walter, 53
Sedgwick, Catherine Maria, 14, 77
Self-interest, 42
Seneca Falls convention (1848), 1
Sentimentalism, 33, 48–50, 54
  see also Romance
Septimus Felton, 4, 6
Sexual abuse, 50

Sexual Politics (Kate Millett), 2, 23–4
Sexuality, female, 12–15, 73, 103–12, 116
Sexuality, literature and, xi–xii
Short stories, 129–30n3
Shurr, W. H., 30
Sibyl Dacy (in *Septimus Felton*), 6
Slavery, 1, 19–20, 126nn61, 62
Snitow, Ann, 12–13
Snow, Caleb, 63
'Snow Image, The', 29–30
Spinsterhood,
  See Hepzibah in The House of the Seven Gables
Stanton, Elizabeth Cady, 31
Stewart, Randall, 52
Stone, Lucy, 31
Stouck, David, 72–3
Suicide, 51, 53
Surveyor Jonathan Pue (in *The Scarlet Letter*), 61–2

Tharp, Louise Hall, 15
Token, The, 57
Tompkins, Jane P., 37–8
Transcendentalism, 10
Twice-told Tales, 57

Unreliable narrator, 99–118
Upham, Charles Wentworth, 82–4

Violence, male, 44–7, 50, 119–21
Von Abele, Rudolph, 114
Voyeurism, 109–10

Waggoner, Hyatt Howe, 52
Walcott (in *Fanshawe*), 42–50
Warren, Joyce W., 13, 25, 36–7
Webster, Noah, 97
Welter, Barbara, 47
Westervelt (*Blithedale Romance*), 112–13, 117
Whipple, E. P., 77
Widows,
  See Elizabeth Hawthorne (his mother), Sophia Hawthorne (his wife), Widow Butler
Widow Butler (in *Fanshawe*), 43
widowhood, 43–4, 51–2, 55
witchcraft, 46, 79–84, 96
Witchcraft trials, 3, 74–5, 79–83
Wizards, 78–84, 96
Woman in the Nineteenth Century (Margaret Fuller), 1, 10–11
Women,
  and abandonment, 41–3
    See also Ellen Langton, Hester Prynne, Phoebe
  and adultery, 63–4, 67–9, 75
    See also Hester Prynne
  attitudes to, 1–22, 87–94, 99–100, 109–12, 117–18,
  as angels, 5, 18, 29, 31–2, 89–91
  and capitalism, 28, 32
  economic status of, 2–3, 133n14
  education of, 1
    See also Una Hawthorne, Elizabeth Peabody
  and feminism, 1–22, 23–38, 100, 104, 107
  in Hawthorne's work, 1–22
    See also under names of individual characters
  and history, 62–4, 66–9, 79–84, 96
  and housework, 89–91, 104–5
  images of, 44–50, 53–4, 59–60, 68–75, 99–118
  legal status of, 2
  and marriage, 17, 20–1, 26, 28, 36, 39, 45–7, 50, 53, 94–6, 119–21
    See Priscilla, Ellen Langton, Phoebe
  as monsters, 30, 46
  and motherhood, 70–1
    See also Hester Prynne
  and persecution as witches, 66–70, 74–5
  and poverty, 2–3, 43, 50–1, 55–6, 84–6, 88

and the professions, 1–2, 13–17
and reform, 6, 65
See also Margaret Fuller, Anne Hutchinson, Elizabeth Peabody, Zenobia
and sexuality, 105–10
and sexual norms, xii, 12–13
single,
See Alice Pyncheon, Ellen Langton, Hepzibah, Hester Prynne, Mistress Hibbins, Priscilla, Zenobia
and theology, 10, 15
See also Anne Hutchinson, Elizabeth Peabody, Hester Prynne
violence against, 44–7, 50, 66–70, 74–5, 119–21
See also Misogyny
and widowhood, 43–4, 51–2, 55
and work, 2–3, 84–7, 88–92
as writers, 7–10, 19, 22
Women's rights, 1, 10, 32–3
Women's Suffrage, 16
Woolf, Virginia, xiii
Writers, women as, 7–10, 19, 22

Yankee and Boston Literary Gazette, 52
'Young Goodman Brown', 3

Zenobia (in *Blithedale Romance*), 5–6, 13, 27–8, 31, 99–113, 115